READING SACRED TEXTS
THROUGH AMERICAN EYES

READING
SACRED TEXTS
THROUGH AMERICAN
EYES

Biblical Interpretation
as Cultural Critique

by
CHARLES MABEE

MERCER

ISBN 0-86554-385-2

Library of Congress Cataloguing-in-Publication Data
Mabee, Charles, 1943–
    Reading sacred texts through american eyes: American biblical her-
meneutics as cultural critique / by Charles Mabee.
    ix + 128 pages 15 x23 cm 6 x 9″
    Includes bibliographical references and index.
    ISBN 0-86554-385-2 (alk. paper)
    1. Bible—Criticism, interpretation, etc.—United States—History. 2.
Theology, Doctrinal—United States—History.   I. Title.
II. Series.
BS500.M22   1991   91-14356
220.6′0973—dc20

For my father, mother, and sister,
who inspired me to think about things American
and things sacred

Deep within them I will plant my Law, writing it on their hearts.
—JEREMIAH 31:33

Here he had studied and written; here, gone through fast and vigil, and come forth half alive; here, striven to pray; here, borne a hundred thousand agonies! There was the Bible, in its rich old Hebrew, with Moses and the Prophets speaking to him, and God's voice through all!
—NATHANIEL HAWTHORNE,
THE SCARLET LETTER

For if men use the green wood like this, what will happen when it is dry?
—LUKE 25:31

Men have come to speak of the revelation as somewhat long ago given and done, as if God were dead.
—RALPH WALDO EMERSON,
"THE DIVINITY SCHOOL ADDRESS"

•CONTENTS•

· ACKNOWLEDGMENTS ·

I am grateful to Marshall University for several research grants that helped make this book possible. I am also very appreciative for the generous help given to me by the staff at Mercer University Press, especially Mr. Edd Rowell and Ms. Susan Carini. Both have encouraged me extensively over the years for both this work and the American Biblical Hermeneutics series in general. Their revisions and suggestions are central to the present form of the book.

Without the support of my wife, Barbara, and my children, Kristin and Jason, this work would never have been completed. Thank all of you very much. I love you.

preTEXT:
American Biblical Hermeneutics
as Cultural Critique

Man lives, not directly or nakedly in nature like the animals, but within a mythological universe, a body of assumptions and beliefs developed from his existential concerns. Most of this is held unconsciously, which means that our imaginations may recognize elements of it, when presented in art or literature, without consciously understanding what it is that we recognize. Practically all that we can see of this body of concern is socially conditioned and culturally inherited. Below the cultural inheritance there must be a common psychological inheritance, otherwise forms of culture and imagination outside our own traditions would not be intelligible to us. But I doubt if we can reach this common inheritance directly, by-passing the distinctive qualities in our specific culture.[1]

The intention of this study is to explore with the reader the means whereby we might read the Bible freshly, to liberate textual voices that have not been heard before in our cultural context. The term *hermeneutics*, as used throughout this work, refers to the problem of understanding *texts*.[2] Since *texts* are read in cultural con*texts*, it is the study of these contexts that clarifies our perception of the meaning of texts, and subse-

---

[1]Northrop Frye, *The Great Code* (New York and London: Harcourt Brace Jovanovich, 1982) xviii.

[2]I am in agreement with Richard Palmer on this point. He writes, "As one tries to distinguish what is specific to hermeneutics, one should say that the 'hermeneutical experience' is first and foremost an encounter with a text—be it dream, a myth, a law, a poem, a novel, or a telegram. Even when philosophical hermeneutics goes beyond this focus on text interpretation it does so in a way that places such interpretation in a more inclusive context." Cf. Richard E. Palmer, "Hermeneutics," in *Contemporary Philosophy: A New Survey*, vol. 2 (The Hague, Boston, London: Martinus Nijhoff, 1982) 459.

quently offers the possibility of a newly discovered critical rereading of the contexts. This is the back and forth movement at play between reader and text that American biblical hermeneutics attempts to analyze. It is the hermeneutical circle of biblical interpretation informed by critical cultural awareness. Furthermore, the critical understanding of the context in which we read the biblical material implies the goal of a fresh reading of the texts. The challenge taken up is this: how can we read the ancient texts of the Bible as if they had not been read before, freeing us from a meaning already predetermined by ecclesiastical, scholarly, and cultural tradition?

We typically think of the problems of textual interpretation in terms of the particular cultural matrixes from which they emerged, rather than in which they are read. This is the result of the scientific spirit of the academy that quests for origins. Practitioners of the historical-critical method are usually content with describing what the biblical text meant in its time and place, and tracing its impact on subsequent periods of history. It is left to the church to bring the meaning of the Bible into both the present situation and the future.[3] To an inordinate degree, however, in America the Bible has operated as a living book within the general cultural context as well as that of the church. Throughout history it has been appealed to as a basic source document by its artists, philosophers, and civil religionists. Americans, it seems, have demanded their own reading of the Bible with as much vitality as have the varied religious communities that have existed in her midst. Here both church and society have maintained a Bible that is a living reality with a present and future meaning, and not simply a past. It is from the task of better understanding this dynamic, organic interplay between text and reader that the reader-oriented hermeneutics of this volume, and the series of which it is a part, has arisen.

A continuing theological issue for our day that remains particularly problematic is the general relationship between religion and culture. At the heart of this problem lies a profound paradox: human culture both makes possible religious experience and hides the deeper realities to which that experience points. The work of interpreting the Bible in dialectical relationship with American culture is intended to liberate the deeper realities of the Bible and our culture for us. To do so means that we must learn to use our culture as a tool to liberate those fragile treasures bequeathed to us from the past. If we are not adept at using our culture, those treasures will remain hidden from our view forever. The hermeneutical circle means that in a sense the whole of the meaning of a text is present in its parts as a "bead of mercury which, even when its original

---

[3]A phrase used by Alfred Whitehead, quoted in Bertrand P. Helm, *Time and Reality in American Philosophy* (Amherst: University of Massachusetts Press, 1985) 191.

mass is shattered, continues in its fractions to manifest the same shape."[4] We already have something of the meaning of any text in the process of encountering it specifically, if only because of the language and thought structures that we bring to it. Thus, the road toward the revitalization of theology is not via the escape of our culture, but the embodying of it self-consciously as we read the Bible, in order to see ourselves more clearly. Theologically we are called to do this because this sort of critical cultural identity was embodied by the writers of the Bible itself. The Bible *is* a critical text within its own cultural milieus and witnesses to a sense of otherness by pointing to the wholly other God. The task of keeping alive this dimension of the Bible in the face of our acculturating domesticity is realizable only by standing in the midst of our own culture and searching for its deeper meanings. It is in this struggle that a biblical hermeneutics peculiar to the American setting is born.

American biblical hermeneutics does not argue for American cultural hegemony, nor hegemony of American ways of reading the Bible. It does not advocate that others read the Bible as Americans do or ought. Rightly done, it should encourage them to read it self-consciously and self-critically within their own cultural context. In this regard, American biblical hermeneutics is indeed universal in scope because it is fundamentally interested in the liberation of the Bible on a worldwide, universal scale. To put the matter succinctly: This way of reading the Bible indicates nothing whatsoever about one's feelings for, or about, America. The myth of the exceptionality and mission of the American experiment itself is a powerful ideology in the modern world. This myth does not merely claim that American life is unique in the world—after all, isn't every culture?—but that it is uniquely unique. America is understood in these especially special terms by virtue of what is termed the American myth, a subject I will discuss more fully below. This myth has become nothing short of a global export that is packaged, sold, imposed upon, appealed to, sought after, rebelled against, and hoped for in soteriological terms. It is important to recognize the complex issues involved in understanding the religious dimension of this cultural experience, and reject the simplistic answers of either pro- or anti-American perspectives. One of the fascinating features of this Americanism is the way it relates to its own foundational texts, among which the Bible exists as a kind of literary nexus. Only by uncovering the nature and depth of our grounding in the American experience can we hope to transcend it in the interpretive process and perhaps

---

[4]Roy J. Howard, *Three Faces of Hermeneutics: An Introduction to Current Theories of Understanding* (Berkeley, Los Angeles, London: University of California Press, 1982) 10. On the same page, Howard goes on to describe the practice of hermeneutics as "a part-whole-part movement, a constant back and forth or dialectical process."

achieve some vantage point from which we may understand both it and the biblical texts themselves anew. Incorporating our particular cultural expression, rather than ignoring it, seems to offer us the possibility of American religious thought achieving a more universal view of God, humanity, and the world in the long run. This approach is *intrinsically* interdisciplinary and dialectical. This book tries to take this aspect of the problem seriously, as will be seen below. It represents the incorporation of the secular into the interpretation of a sacred book. The democratic/ capitalistic environment in which we live demands that this step be taken. Failure to do so results in increasing loss of relevancy of our religious traditions in the marketplace of ideas, and the posturing of religion as a salable commodity designed to uphold the status quo.

A primary intention of this book is to explore how the Bible might be liberated from the exclusive realm of ecclesiastical interpretation and interjected on its own terms into the mainstream of public life. Vibrant theology has always been stimulated by forces of secularity, but the well-documented boundary between the sacred and the secular is often difficult to find in America. Yet, the secular culture in which we live—taken as a whole—has staked its own claims upon the Bible quite apart from the American religious institutions whose freedoms are safeguarded by it. The pragmatic, utilitarian orientation of American life has tended to cast a utilitarian image over the Bible. The result has been the loss of critical spirit. The exposition of American biblical hermeneutics, therefore, becomes doubly important and doubly difficult in this particular culture. A fundamental theological task today is to determine critically what is authentically sacred in our way of life and cultural mythos, and what is not. This is the starting point for American biblical hermeneutics and the public hermeneutics that it implies.

We are all aware that the Bible is the product of believing religious communities; it is fundamentally a religious text. At the same time, the American cultural milieu, bequeathed to us in part by the forces of modernity with its relatively neat distinctions between sacred and profane, exists as something quite foreign to biblical cultures and texts. The call for a public biblical hermeneutics[5] is in essence a call for the establishment of a holistic view of religion—a new way of integrating sacred text and public culture that retains the critical spirit of each. The simple fact is that we

---

[5] As I hope becomes clear throughout the course of this book, I am in basic agreement with Reinhold Niebuhr, Martin Marty, David Tracy, and others who advocate a strong public dimension of theology. Tracy, for example, writes, "All theology is public discourse. . . . Theologians do not only recognize a plurality of 'publics' to whom they intend to speak, but also more and more the theologians are internalizing this plurality in their own discourse." In *The Analogical Imagination: Christian Theology and the Culture of Pluralism* (New York: Crossroad, 1981) 3–5.

must subject the Christian faith to the forces of democracy if it is to survive in a democratic society—and democracy derives its authority from
the people, not prescriptively from either clerics or academics. This public, democratic hermeneutics incorporates within the interpretive process
the recognition that while many biblical texts were preserved and carried
through the ages in the context of orthodox religious institutions, the
original voices of the Bible carried implications for all members of society.
In a helpful way, David Tracy recently delineated three distinct components of the theological public when he wrote: "Each theologian addresses three distinct and related social realities: the wider society, the
academy and the church."[6] The public reading of the Bible that I am sug-
gesting encompasses all three of these communal structures. The implication of this approach is that to make of the Bible simply a book of the
believing community is to limit severely the vitality of its texts. If the Bible
is only the book of the church, it will have failed the acid test of democratic life.

The specific way the Bible has functioned authoritatively for the
American experience rests upon historical fact, rather than theological
prescription. In fact, it has been, and continues to be, the standard or norm
by which we historically judge ourselves. A product of other cultures, it
is yet the bearer of our own deepest societal aspirations. Thus, granted
that it is theologically risky to move the Bible from the secure prescriptive
arms of the church, it is a risk our society calls for. In point of fact, from
an exclusively ecclesiastical point of view, the Bible lies very much con-
cealed, frequently serving only to prop up lifeless and domesticated ecclesiastical theologies whose roots are European, not American. And,
while biblical study is more alive in our academic settings, it functions
there all too frequently as the exclusive property of an elite who define
themselves in primarily secular terms. The social and political events of
our time give witness to the enormous appeal of underwriting the status
quo through reference to commonly held ideas of what the Bible says, but
this appeal shows remarkably little hermeneutical sophistication and
wrestling with actual biblical texts. A public reading of the Bible addresses this problem by incorporating ongoing ecclesiastical and academic interpretive communities while moving beyond them to issues of
common cultural concern. It is, after all, the impulse of democracies to
make public those things that previous societies have held restrictively or
secretively.

With these initial observations about American biblical hermeneutics
now set forth, it may be useful to lay out in summary form certain theoretical implications of the public reading of the Bible in America. As I understand them, I may summarize the more important as follows:

---

[6]Ibid., 5.

1. American biblical hermeneutics is grounded in a relational way of thinking that offers the possibility of reading biblical texts in a fresh way that we might term a *hermeneutics of engagement*. Engagement implies at least two independent, particular entities; and it is from the interaction between these two that the possibility of fresh readings exist. In this case, the two entities are the biblical text and those traditions that shape its American reader. It is the ever-changing horizon of meaning brought to the text by its readers that continually reinvigorates and revitalizes the text. American biblical hermeneutics specifically inquires into the theological meaning to be won in the interaction between them. It does not attempt to synthesize these two intellectual horizons; rather, it maintains the independent integrity of both the biblical text and the cultural realities that shape the worldview of the reader, and situates both of them in the hermeneutical circle. On the one hand, this approach implies a renewed commitment to the otherness of the text and the world that produced it; but just as importantly, it establishes the independent reality of the reader, and the cultural ethos that he/she brings to the reading experience. Therefore, the difference that exists between text and reader is not lost between the "fusion of horizons" that takes place in the hermeneutical process.[7] In fact, this difference between reader and text is a sine qua non for the hermeneutics of engagement and is maintained throughout the process of interpretation.

This tension of concurrent horizons operative between text and reader means that American biblical hermeneutics maintains a priority of the particular and concrete over the universal and abstract. This element of particularity is maintained by means of its explicit focus on the specific entities of *Bible* and *American* reader. The hallmark of this activity is particular *texts* in particular *contexts*. Presupposed is the perspective that the human condition itself is grounded in forms of particularity rather than universality. The promise of such an approach is manifold. The particularity of text and context provides a constant safeguard against the imposition of universal theological prescription upon any particular cultural setting. The history of Western civilization teaches us that we must protect secular society from the encroachment of the church just as vigilantly as we must protect the church from the encroachment of secular society.

---

[7]On this point, Hans-Georg Gadamer writes, "Every encounter with tradition that takes place within historical consciousness involves the experience of the tension between the text and the present. The hermeneutic task consists in not covering up this tension by attempting a naive assimilation but consciously bringing it out. This is why it is part of the hermeneutical approach to project an historical horizon that is different from the horizon of the present. Historical consciousness is aware of its own otherness and hence distinguishes the horizon of tradition from its own." In Gadamer, *Truth and Method* (New York: Seabury Press, 1975) 273.

In American biblical hermeneutics, engagement replaces prescription. Furthermore, this particularistic thrust of American biblical hermeneutics points to a plurality of contextual readings of the Bible, rather than one definitive reading. However, as I shall argue in the main body of this study, it seems to me that practitioners of American biblical hermeneutics need ultimately to strive beyond this plurality of readings for a grammar of cultural understanding that undergirds the way the Bible is read in American life, regardless of the particular cultural subgroup. Laying bare the common grammar that envelops our reading of the Bible is what makes this work specifically theological, and not simply exegetical. *American Biblical Hermeneutics* implies a new way of understanding the meaning of those methods of exegesis we already employ. In this way it is an exegesis of exegesis, even as it is a hermeneutic of hermeneutics.

Exegetically, it is not possible or desirable to remove the Hebrew cultural environment from the Old Testament, nor to extract primitive Christianity from Hellenistic civilization. The biblical writers themselves teach us that the particularity of human experience is a necessary partner to universal thought, and an ongoing corrective to it, in spite of frequent attempts by kings, prophets, priests, and scholars to displace it with universal rules and prescriptions. As dominant strands of contemporary philosophical and hermeneutical theory inform us, the task is to come into full awareness of our subjectivity, not to overcome it. All vital theological discourse is embedded in this specificity of our lives, and continually directed to it for sustenance and nourishment. The Christian faith is called upon to articulate itself in universal terms, but this is a universality similarly grounded in the particularities of cultural existence. To deny this is to deny the fleshliness of human existence that is thrown into a particular place and time in the drama of human history. It is to deny the essence of the American democratic experiment.

2. The engagement of cultural ethos explicitly into the reading process results in the primacy of praxis in theological discourse over theory and abstraction. Don Ihde has recently discussed the issue of the priority of *praxical knowledge* over *theoretical knowledge*.[8] While the approach taken in this book is partly representative of the inherent American distrust for "pure theory," it is more the nature of the ontological implications of "American biblical hermeneutics" itself that force to the forefront this axiom: "Religion is *praxis* before it is *theoria*."[9] In this activity all theoretical

---

[8]Don Ihde, *Technics and Praxis* (Dordrecht, Holland: D. Reidel, 1976) xxiv–xxv.

[9]Harold H. Oliver, *Relatedness: Essays in Metaphysics and Theology* (Macon GA: Mercer University Press, 1984) 163. Oliver continues: "Such verbs, or actions, as 'worshiping,' 'praying,' 'praising,' 'sacrificing,' uniquely represent religious *praxis*. One of the great truths of our Tradition is that devotion to an object—even to one considered Divine—is not worship, but idolatry. I can best express my central claim

reflection is situated in the engagement of particular texts with the determinative forces of cultural existence.

This grounding of our interpretive efforts in praxis aids us in the restoration of the vitality of the Bible in both our ecclesiastical and public lives. Grounded in the cultural realities of everyday existence, American biblical hermeneutics establishes those fundamental theological ties that exist between the praxis of the reader and the praxis that generated the text (whether in historical or functional terms). Thus, American biblical hermeneutics is not simply situated in a dialectical otherness of text and reader, but in an otherness that is defined by praxis. A praxical approach to the Bible begins with the questioning of the text for its own response to everyday issues of cultural existence. For example, we might inquire into those ways that the experience of kingship, interpreted from the perspective of exile, shaped the Deuteronomistic History. How is this experience of kingship to be compared and contrasted with that reflected in the Yahwistic source? Or, again, does the Gospel of Matthew reflect an intimate experience with the Judaism it critiques? Innumerable historical-critical questions of similar orientation abound in the biblical corpus. Biblical hermeneutics takes an important step beyond such specific issues of biblical criticism, however, and inquires into the ways in which these biblical experiences are relevant for real-life, contemporary situations. What are the theological implications of such perspectives for the modern world? How does one translate perspectives and concerns that are no longer evident? Conversely, how does one move credibly from contemporary problematical experiences to the world of the Bible in which such experiences were nonexistent? But, most important, how does modern cultural experience help us uncover new meanings within the biblical texts? Such an approach to the Bible is sensitive to the concerns of historical criticism, yet does not undermine the vitality of the religious experience itself.

Theoretical studies in hermeneutics are in much evidence today. Their contribution to our understanding of the problematical aspects of textual reading is enormous, the effect of which will mount in the years ahead. Yet, this discipline seems peculiarly afflicted with the methodological biases that afflict the academy in our time. So much is written about the hermeneutical study of texts that the more creative of such studies frequently become primary texts in their own right, displacing the texts they are intended to elucidate. Arguably, the writings of Ricoeur and Gada-

---

by adapting the subtitle of an article which I came across. . . . :
    To the non-religious, the term 'God' is a noun;
    To the religious, God is a verb."

mer fall into this category.[10] Such contributions enlighten us greatly about the theoretical dimensions of understanding texts. American biblical hermeneutics redirects this movement toward disembodied theorizing back toward the actual engagement of texts. By anchoring hermeneutical interests to the specific poles of Bible (text) and American culture (reader), theory is continually concretized. The benefits of this approach enhance both the intellectual activity of hermeneutics itself and the understanding of the American religious experience. It is in such a practical context that hermeneutics must prove itself. In short, hermeneutical theory must make a difference in the actual reading of texts if it is to maintain its legitimacy.

3. The concretizing element of a public biblical hermeneutics leads to a redefined way of viewing the canonicity of the Bible. This is an opposing position to that argued by Brevard Childs, one I have discussed elsewhere.[11] Childs makes an interesting attempt to escape the contemporary methodological uncertainties that exist in historical-critical biblical studies by shifting the locus of interpretation from historical scholarship to the believing community. This shift is not made at the expense of the historical-critical methodologies, but is intended theologically to incorporate and transcend them. Yet, I maintain that Childs has not succeeded in extricating biblical studies from the objectivism or scientism that he intends. Rather, he has only relocated the reductionism of historical criticism. In order for the Bible to regain a meaningful relevance for our time and place, it is necessary to go beyond such ecclesiastical limitations. It is certainly not propitious to relinquish the gains achieved by post-Enlightenment criticism. Now is not the time to reinforce the already problematical separation of community of faith / community of humankind.

Embedded in the term *canon* is the ecclesiastically based concept of the revelation. In particular, the problematic feature of this perspective is that it implies the absolute superiority of a particular text over all other texts. This can only be done on the basis of ecclesiastical authority. The potential of exploiting this concept for institutional gain is great. The democratic American cultural context requires a theological perception of the Bible that moves from this static concept to a more dynamic one captured in a less absolutizing term, such as *revealedness*. Rather than predicating absolute truths about God based upon this or that biblical text (the revelation), theologians are called upon to recognize that any "uncovering" of truth must assume a particular form that is subject to the delimitations of the cultural matrix of the one-to-whom-it-is-revealed. The prescriptive

---

[10]For an excellent discussion of this point, see the introductory essay in Gary Shapiro and Alan Sica, eds., *Hermeneutics: Questions and Prospects* (Amherst: University of Massachusetts Press, 1984).

[11]Cf. Charles Mabee, *Reimagining America* (Macon GA: Mercer University Press, 1985) 24–27.

concept of revelation is grounded in institutional claims of canonicity; the dialogical concept of revealedness claims scripture or sacred text set apart that retains the human pole in dialectical relation to specific ecclesiastical claims. The former view tends to absolutize biblical texts by thrusting them authoritatively into the theological future: it establishes the a priori parameters of what God's activity will be in the world.[12] The interests and concerns of the institutionalized church dominate in this theological future. In a word, the canonical view of biblical interpretation is propagandistic in intentionality. In this context, the Bible tends to serve the purpose of explaining the raison d'être of institutional life and practices as it is employed by the church.

The approach of American biblical hermeneutics is open-ended and searching. It is a-canonical in the sense that it *requires* the experience of the reader to complement the experience of the biblical author as a prerequisite to theological discourse. It is, therefore, grounded in the traditio-historical recognition that the subjective concerns of faith from generation to generation are formative in the production of biblical texts. For this reason, the interpretation of the Bible is set in the context of the broader American cultural experience in an effort to follow up the traditio-historical implications of the formation of biblical texts. Much Western intellectual history, American intellectual history included, represents a protest against a reductionistic ecclesiastical exclusivity. The reduction of a real voice in the vital intellectual centers of our civilization is the natural result of a too narrowly conceived interpretive approach. Interpretive schemes that limit the locus of interpretation to the institutional community of faith, and the apologetic stratagem of canonicity that it employs, results in a truncated reading that obscures the Bible's own claim for universal meaning. It is true that the Bible is the product of the believing community, but the writers of the Bible make no claim that this community contains the totality of the object of their belief.[13] For them,

---

[12]Note the excellent discussion in Gerald L. Bruns, "Canon and Power," in Robert von Hallberg, ed., *Canons* (Chicago and London: University of Chicago Press, 1984) 65–83. Note the reference to time in the following statement by Bruns: "The whole point of canonization is to underwrite the authority of a text, not merely with respect to its origin as against competitors in the field—this, technically, would simply be a question of authenticity—*but with respect to the present and future in which it will reign or govern as a binding text*" [my emphasis]. He continues, "From a hermeneutical standpoint, in which the relation of a text to a situation is always of primary interest, the theme of canonization is *power*" [author's emphasis]. Cf. p. 67.

[13]Cf. David L. Bartlett, *The Shape of Scriptural Authority* (Philadelphia: Fortress, 1983). Bartlett argues that "the church provides the context in which the canon is interpreted" (149). My review of Bartlett's book appears in *Interpretation* 34:3 (July 1985): 330–31.

Yahweh fully emerged as the creator of the entire *world* in the course of the development of its traditions—not simply Israel, or the Christian church. Indeed, the possibility of the existence of Israel or the Christian church is eventually seen only as a possibility against the backdrop of a "theology of world" (creation + preservation). We might portray the matter in this way: The writers of the Bible gave substance and intelligibility to their subjective faith communities upon the objective ground of a theology of world. This hermeneutical strategy to establish Christian theology upon such an objective foundation is perhaps the most far-reaching theological decision to be made by the early church.[14] I maintain that it is of greater importance, for example, than the centuries-long Christological struggles that succeeded it. The Christological controversies themselves derive much of their sustenance from the theology of world and are by and large predicated upon it. It seems to me that the same perspective must inform our own interpretative efforts.

4. The hermeneutics of engagement leads to a fundamental reformulation of theology within the American context. American biblical hermeneutics is fundamentally a theological discipline and does not fit neatly into sociological, anthropological, historical, or cultural disciplines. That notion implies that it draws upon the insights of such studies and that these disciplines, as they bear upon this subject, are brought to the bar of theological judgment and evaluation. Thus, the terminology American / biblical / hermeneutics is not exclusively concerned with America, the Bible, or hermeneutics. Rather, it is occupied with the work of theological reflection, namely, the nature of God and religious truth. In fact, it seems to me that one of the primary aims of American biblical hermeneutics is to resist the vaporization of theology into all other "logia." If nothing else, the biblical component in the terminology will simply not allow this to happen. It opens the possibility of a critical critique of the received Christian tradition from the vantage point of American ethos. The methodological otherness that American biblical hermeneutics maintains between biblical text and American reader carries with it theological implications of the highest order.

The hermeneutics of cultural engagement is historically grounded in the theological problem of the precise definition of the relationship between the culturally divergent Old and New Testaments. This issue goes back to the earliest Christian traditions. This potential hostility at play in these divergent collections of texts is ameliorated by the tradition by means of the chronological terminology *old* and *new*. By bracketing out this subsequently imposed chronological schema, and maintaining the inherently distinctive Hebrew and Greek cultural tensions in the spirit of American cultural diversity, a theological path is opened whereby the in-

---

[14]This perspective was worked out in the early encounter with Gnosticism.

tentionality of the entire Christian Bible is made in terms of the underlying faith in Yahweh as the one, true God of the universe. Failure to accept
this diversity means that the Bible remains captive to the received tradition of European Christianity. The textual bond between the Testaments
can only be established meaningfully on the basis of Yahweh, because
Jesus is present in the Old Testament only on the basis of faith. Whether
and how to read Jesus back into the Old Testament is a risk-taking venture that must be considered anew by each generation of biblical readers,
because of the violence that it implies to Old Testament texts. To read
Yahweh into the New Testament does not imply this same sort of violence, indeed the texts themselves demand it as part of their presuppo-
sitional context. To put this another way: An ecclesiastical reading of the
Bible tends toward imposing Jesus upon the texts of the Old Testament;
whereas, a public reading tends toward uncovering Yahweh as the pre-
suppositional God of the New Testament. This is the theological starting
point for a public American biblical hermeneutics that recognizes the fundamental place of particular cultural diversity.

Based in part on a strong Calvinistic heritage, American theologians
have typically been unsatisfied with an overly drawn theological chasm
erected between the Old and New Testaments. We may further state the
matter this way: the *division* between the Old and New Testaments is an
ecclesiastical one, while the *distinction* between them is a cultural (public)
one. By bringing them into relation to one another, while retaining their
individual integrity, it becomes clear that Yahwism is not fundamentally
altered by this chronological distinction of *Old* and *New*. Theologically,
we might say that the transtestamental perspectives found in Exodus and
John reflect no greater divergence than those found within the Hebrew
Scriptures themselves, for example between Deuteronomy and Job. The
Old Testament, in other words, exhibits the capacity to maintain a plurality of perspectives under its own roof that manifests a theological di-
versity as great as, if not greater than, that which exists between the Old
and New Testaments. The path of the solution to the problem of the two
Testaments lies, it seems to me, precisely along the lines that the hermeneutical approach of this book follows. In a slightly different context, Harold
H. Oliver makes the same point about the historical relationship between
Judaism and Christianity that I am attempting to sketch out here. He writes,
"The earliest insight that Jesus was a paradigm of what is true quickly de-
teriorated into a nonrelational Christology, thus creating the ontological
chasm between Judaism and Christianity. In a relational theology the dis-
tinctiveness of both Judaism and Christianity continues to be affirmed, but
it is based on their diverse historical particularity rather than on an ontolog-
ically different affirmation."[15] Exactly the same point could be made about

---

[15]Oliver, *Relatedness*, 18–19.

the relation of the two Testaments: they are based on the same ontological ground of faith in Yahweh, even though they must always be distinguished on the grounds of historical particularity. This theological proposition is a natural unfolding of the same morphology of relationship existing between American reader and biblical text. Each of these categories must be distinguished from the other, but they are correctly set within a context of prior mutuality. It is commonly recognized in the contemporary discussion of biblical theology that each of the Testaments contains more than a single theology. Old Testament theology in particular has shown us the complex interrelationships of the textuality of Yahwism. This plurality of biblical theologies has a number of implications for the Christian faith. This includes the necessity of relating them systematically, as, for example, Rolf Knierim does in his reflections on Old Testament theology under the vantage point of "the universal dominion of Yahweh in justice and righteousness,"[16] and the perennial search for the canon within the canon. But prior to any such systematic work is the theological imperative to interpret the fact that the Bible itself structurally makes room for this plurality of theological perspectives by virtue of the Old/New Testament distinction.

5. American biblical hermeneutics implies the extension of the critical spirit utilized in the study of biblical material into the realm of the reader. There exists both an intrinsic, or internal, and a referential, or external, dimension to the reader's horizon. In the American setting, I believe it is most insightful to term the forces shaping the internal aspect *mythological*, and those constituting the external *technological*. I will discuss these briefly in turn in the final two points of this discussion. Myth has been studied in twentieth century scholarship in divergent ways. The work that remains to be completed is the turning of our tools for the interpretation of myth back upon ourselves as readers. It is instructive, therefore, to consider specifically the so-called American myth as it relates to biblical texts. I will return to this critical subject below, but several introductory observations are appropriate here. The contours of this myth are well known, having been the subject of a wealth of scholarly activity in recent years, often under the rubric of American civil religion.[17] Such ideas as manifest destiny, the work ethic and concomitant economic rewards, an overriding sense of optimism and confidence, the conception of the New Adam in the New Garden, and the pursuit of happiness are all grounded in this myth. Much of the American story can be reduced to the perpetual

---

[16]Cf. Rolf Knierim, "The Task of Old Testament Theology," in *Horizons in Biblical Theology* 6:1 (1984): 25–57.

[17]For a comprehensive discussion of the American myth, cf. Sacvan Bercovitch, *The Puritan Origins of the American Self* (New Haven and London: Yale University Press, 1975) esp. 136–86.

struggle to realize these postulates of the American Dream.

The question for American biblical hermeneutics is how to approach this mythic substratum of the American psyche after engaging the biblical texts. Above all, it is evident that the biblical writers were engaged in a demythologization project of their own in ancient Israel as that society grappled with the various mythologies that it encountered beyond its own cultural bounds (Canaanite, Babylonian, Egyptian, Hellenistic, and the like). We can see from the residue of these encounters that still exist in the Bible that the biblical texts drive to the underlying ground of myth and inquire into the contextual implications of it for the faith broadly conceived. For example, when Yahwism encountered the nature gods of Canaan, it did not deny the necessity of religion's encompassing legitimate agricultural concerns. While it forced the people to stand outside their nature mythologies to choose either Baal or Yahweh, it affirmed the reason for those mythologies even as it rejected much of the specific mythological content. The same point might be made with regard to the royal Zion mythology viewed in the context of more elaborate royal theologies of the ancient Near East, as well as in the impact of Hellenistic religion upon the theological model of Paul. Demythologization, yes, but not simply demythologization. This is a demythologization process that is sympathetic to the underlying concerns and activities that gave rise to the mythologies in the first place. Acknowledging these concerns gave the opportunity for an expanded view of the activity of Yahweh in the world. It was a benevolent demythologization program that allowed for and encouraged restricted mythology to exist within established theological guidelines.

As one embarks upon the task of approaching American myth in an analogous fashion to the way the biblical writers interpreted the myth of their day, one is struck by the fact that it is also by and large a product of other cultures, in this case European. All the essential components of that myth, including those noted above, have their roots in the Old World. The concept of "the American experiment," for example, achieves its overriding significance only in the context of European hopes and expectations. The opening up of American lands to European immigrants represented an opportunity for the incarnation of European culture that circumstances had by and large denied them at home. It was the opportunity to actually live out European dreams and aspirations, unencumbered by the social and geographical limitations of the Continent, that generated the New World mythos. Obviously, the New World was not new at all. From the standpoint of natural history, it was extremely ancient. Even from the perspective of Native Americans (the unfortunates who could not share the American myth), it was hardly new. The newness of America was something to be seen only from the standpoint of European culture. We might say that "America" as an intellectual construction was intimately bound up with the radical manipulation of time and space from the beginning. This fact helps bring content to the structure of the symbiotic relationship that has existed between Europe and America from precolonial times to the present. For America, Europe is conceived as the source of her leading ideas, indeed, of those ideas that give force and validity to the very meaning of herself. To be cut off from the ground of those ideas is to be cast adrift in a sea of ambiguous loss of identity (note, in recent history, the seeming loss of purpose characteristic of American activities in Southeast Asia and the aggressive attempt to reseize purpose in the Persian Gulf). For Europe, on the other hand, America stands as the one opportunity for the self-realization that has proven so elusive on the Continent itself.

The encounter with the Bible makes it imperative that the American mythos be seen more critically and realistically in the process of reader demythologization, as a prerequisite for understanding. Again, while the more compelling biblical traditions do not demand the end of all myth (for they themselves contain myth), time and again they do demand that one face up to one's own myth as myth. In other words, from this perspective, myth must have what Paul Tillich calls the "capacity for self-negation."[18] Myth that does not have this capacity is idolatrous. The Old Testament is particularly rich in examples of this basic perspective: for example, the self-negations of its own royal ideologies (1 Samuel 9ff.) and Wisdom traditions (Job, Ecclesiastes), in addition to those passages that rebuke human reason by attributing a demonic-like character to Yahweh (Exodus 4:24, 1 Kings 22:19–23). As its Wisdom traditions indicate, Israel came to view an uncritical mythology as leading to spiritual and intellectual impotence. As such, no true encounter with God could take place apart from the willingness to forego the absoluteness of one's own myth. Such willingness is the true entrée into an authentic dialectical encounter with the Bible. Both Israel and the early church engaged in a sustained dialogue with their cultural peers and found this to be an enervating and dynamic experience. But such an encounter was always undertaken without loss of self-identity or critical perspective on the part of biblical writers. To obscure the claims that the Bible makes on us *before* it allows us to become responsive to it is not hermeneutics, it is antihermeneutics. One of the primary tasks of American biblical hermeneutics is to establish the extent of those claims operative in this cultural setting defined by pervasive technology and to contribute to the creative theological encounter that may be extracted from it. Only in this way may the biblical text be truly liberated and given the opportunity for a fruitful exchange with us. A realistic appraisal of one's own mythology is the necessary complement to the historical-critical exegetical methodologies that have provided us with so much helpful data about the meaning of the biblical texts in their historical environment.

---

[18]See Paul Tillich, *Dynamics of Faith* (New York: Harper & Row, 1957).

6. Finally, I will conclude this opening discussion of American biblical hermeneutics with reference to the external or referential expression of our cultural life that has most profoundly fleshed out the American myth in a material way, namely, the pervasive technological aspect of our cultural self-definition.[19] Certainly America is a complex, pluralistic society that befuddles any reductionistic attempts at definition.[20] Yet, I am convinced by those who argue that American pluralism is generally co-opted by the dominant, prevailing technological culture. The point is that we can be pluralistic only to the extent that the undergirding technological system itself remains secure and maintains its integrity. In this way, American pluralism is primarily mediated to the culture as a whole through the manipulative powers of technological reasoning. For this reason, I maintain the primacy of technology, and not pluralism, as a more primary intellectual category for American biblical hermeneutics. This book will argue that technological thinking offers us hermeneutical access to the paradox symbiosis of religion and culture as it is manifest in our time and place. My thesis is that *the study of technology stands as an especially fruitful portal of entry into problems associated with reading the Bible in American culture because the diversity of American readings of the Bible all take place in the space assigned them by the dominance of modern technology.* By centering on the workings of technology in American culture, and utilizing it as a means of evolving new meaning from our reading of the Bible, I hope to show concretely that absorbing the secular into the hermeneutical process breathes new life and spirit into our understanding of the Bible. To be either anti- or protechnological in this environment is beside the point. If we are to reimagine who we are and what we might become, then our imagination must be anchored to the technological realities we now embody. Any other option, such as the denial or dismantling of these technological realities, is unthinkable. The path to a public reading of the

---

[19]I am in agreement with George Grant, when he writes, "We live, then, in the most realized technological society which has yet been; one which is, moreover, the chief imperial center from which technique is spread around the world. It might seem, then, that because we are destined so to be, we might also be the people best able to comprehend what it is to be so. Because we are first and most fully there, the need might seem to press upon us to try to know where we are in this new-found land which is so obviously a 'terra incognita.' Yet the very substance of our existing which has made us the leaders in technique, stands as a barrier to any thinking which might be able to comprehend technique from beyond its own dynamism." In Grant, "Technology and Empire," in Carl Mitcham and Robert Mackey, eds., *Philosophy and Technology: Readings in the Philosophical Problems of Technology* (New York: Free Press, 1983) 200.

[20]Michael Kammen terms American culture "an *unstable* pluralism" (author's emphasis) and the "contrapuntal civilization." In *People of Paradox* (New York, Toronto: Oxford University Press, 1980) 60 and chap. 9.

Bible is carved out of the American wilderness by the forces of technological enterprise, and to read the Bible publically is to keep those technological realities in view.

Because of the immense problems associated with American technology, and the broad sweep of problems that come into our consciousness
with it, I think that it is realistic to speak of a *technological burden* for the
religious traditions that have flourished in American life. By that I mean
that the various religions operative in this cultural context have had demands made upon them that greatly exceed the traditional meanings of
their fundamental texts. No one has seen this with more clarity than the
nineteenth-century observer of America society Alexis de Tocqueville, a
thinker whose work will occupy us at the beginning of the main section
of this book. The attractiveness of technology in America (and increasingly the world), and the rational techniques of social order that are inspired by it, are best understood against the backdrop of the unstable
elements of cultural and political pluralism. Religion, within this environment, tends to be reduced primarily to the function of supporting the
prevailing system. Thus, the study of American ethos leads eventually to
the preeminence of one particular theoretical problem: our failure to come
to an adequate understanding of the technological impulse that dominates within it with relative impunity. Crèvecoeur's New Man is not simply infatuated with technology;[21] he comes to embody it as no other people
in the world. Nowhere else has the technological/scientific mentality been
structured into the very fabric of society as in America. Many have pointed
to the religiosity and piety of Americans, but rarely do these phenomena
stand independent of or in critical relationship to the technological milieu
that has been created here. This technology tends to be inclusive rather
than exclusive. That is to say, it supports and defends itself by techniques
of co-option, rather than suppression. In so doing, it is tolerant of an ex-
traordinarily wide variety of human experiences—tolerant insofar as these
experiences may be adapted and transformed into the prevailing system.

The emergence of technology as the dominant cultural force in America has arisen partly in response to the excess of its pluralistic subcultural
traditions. The European intellectual traditions that generated the discovery and settlement of America were no match for the cultural pluralism that was encountered on the North American continent. This was true
of the mix of the various European cultures that found their way to this
place; it was all the more true when Native American, African, Asian,
Eastern, and Near Eastern traditions were added to the mix. The result

---

[21]Although convinced of the goodness of American soil, Crèvecoeur nevertheless adds, "Sometimes I delight in inventing and executing machines, which
simplify my wife's labor." In J. Hector St. John de Crèvecoeur, *Letters from an
American Farmer* (New York: E. P. Dutton, 1957) 33.

was that not one single cultural tradition was capable of rising to a position of dominance in America. Instead, the technological tradition itself—the marrow of the skeleton of the amalgamated European traditions that had originally conceptualized the image of "America" and had brought it into existence—was instituted as the new American ideology. It became the integrative force binding together a multivocal civilization. The texts I have selected to interpret illustrate this point.

This very same spirit of technology that had discovered the New World and populated its shores, would in the course of historical development be turned inward upon the continent itself, upon its land and the life of its people. The plurality of cultures that populated America were themselves profoundly transformed in this development. German cultural expression in America, for example, was different than the very same expression in Germany itself. The same may be said for African culture, or whatever other example one chooses. This difference lay in something much more profound than a change in geographical climate or the impact of the various traditions upon one another. The most profound change the new environment brought upon the traditional cultures was its interpretation of them as excess. This becomes clearer when we realize that those engaged in the formation of the dominant American technological society were themselves in effect employing a cultural hermeneutics of the various American subgroups. Again, the fundamental hermeneutical problem to be overcome was the one of overwhelming cultural diversity. The basic strategy employed was that which transformed the various vital subcultural American traditions into traditions of excess. That which was interpreted as excess could be far more easily removed as a threat to the unification of the culture as a whole. To be cast in the intellectual mold of excess meant that any claims to ultimacy, which any or all of the subgroups might make, were de facto eliminated. The distinction Heidegger makes between *correctness* and *truth* is appropriate here: any particular cultural subgroup in America might be correct in its limited goals and aspirations, but only the supraculture of technology offered the possibility for truth itself to emerge to the culture as a whole.[22] The association of an almost unlimited confidence in a technological worldview, and a developing mythos of exceptionality and mission, stands as a cultural monument to the power and vitality of the emerging world power manifest in the twentieth century.

The priority given action and experientially based philosophies in the American intellectual tradition is fueled by the confusing conflux of traditions that populated the cultural mix. This complex, plural cultural base

---

[22]" . . . the merely correct is not yet the true." Martin Heidegger, "The Question Concerning Technology," in *Martin Heidegger: Basic Writings,* ed. David Krell (New York: Harper & Row, 1977) 289.

simply exceeds the capacities of the inherited intellectual paradigms. Philosophical pragmatism is one result of this phenomenon, just as is literary realism and the New Criticism. More important for our considerations, Continental theology, whether in Southern or Northern European formulations, was similarly unequal to the American experience. As a result, both Catholicism and Protestantism, for example, tend to live increasingly off their common activity in the American cultural context, rather than the originally divisive conflicts of their European heritage. In this regard, American fundamentalism stands as a major intellectual effort to match the dominant American technological experience with the Christian faith, by cutting away the excess of the European theological traditions. Rightly understood, this fundamentalism stands on similar ground with pragmatism, scientism, and literary realism. Its reemergence as a dominant force in American life in our own generation is not surprising. At its heart, fundamentalism is reductionistic. Again, we might borrow Heidegger's distinction: it is much easier to argue the *correctness* of the fundamentalistic impulse than its *truthfulness*. Part of the difficulty seems to lie in the fact that it is conceived and nurtured as a negative reaction to modernity in general and American cultural plurality in particular. Fundamentalism is correct in its critique of the surplus of the inherited European traditions, but it departs too quickly from the praxis of the American setting. As such, left to itself, it tends to become dogmatized in ways that excessively distort and delimit the range of religious experience.

The goal of American biblical hermeneutics lies in the transformation of religion from a static object of predicated theology to that of a dynamic realm of experience. In order for this to occur, it is necessary to transform the complexities of American cultural pluralism from its conceptualization as *excess*, unable to fit within the narrow theological framework of the inherited European theologies, to that of fundamental *resource*. Only in this way can American theological reflection be worthy of the name. Moreover, I believe that this work of transformation is the basic contribution that theology itself can play in American life. What other institutionally related activity can bring this transformation into effect? In metaphorical terms, I might say that the task of religious thought in America is to restore intelligible speech to the Babel of Tongues represented in its cultural diversity. In this sense the task is spiritual, for only the spirit can weave its way through the complexities of the problem before us. But this spirituality must have a very visible rational infrastructure, for the work must derive from our understanding of ourselves in the world in which we live, be intelligible to us, and guide us in the challenges of our age.

conTEXT:
American Reader

The first charm and virgin promise of America were that it was so different a place. But the fulfillment of modern America would be its power to level time and places, to erase differences between here and there, between now and then. And finally the uniqueness of America would prove to be its ability to erase uniqueness.

Elsewhere democracy had meant forms of personal, political, economic, and social equality. In the United States, in addition, there would be a novel environmental democracy. Here, as never before, the world would witness the "equalizing" of times and places.

The flavor of life had once come from winter's cold, summer's heat, the special taste and color of each season's diet. The American Democracy of Times and Places meant making one place and one thing more like another, by bringing them under the control of man.[1]

• Introduction •

American biblical hermeneutics engages the Bible from the standpoint of primary texts that lay bare the interior topology of American ethos. By the term *interior*, I mean that part of the American experience that lies hidden beneath the surface of everyday existence but is presupposed by it. The texts that I have chosen to read are not merely descriptive, but intend to uncover that ethos at its most fundamental level of meaning. These texts point to a kind of progressive *cultural grammar* of the American way of perceiving the world: a trajectory of thought that runs from the kind of democratic despotism feared by Tocqueville in the early to mid-nineteenth century to the emergence of the autonomous technology recently depicted by Jacques Ellul. Other texts could be chosen to make the same essential argument, but these writings are particularly insightful and

---

[1]Daniel Boorstin, *The Americans: The Democratic Experience* (New York: Vintage, 1974) 307.

penetrating. My argument is that this trajectory represents a kind of grammar of thought that necessarily underlies a public reading of the Bible in American culture.

This grammar of thought lies beneath the theological register of discourse that characterizes our more thoughtful religious reflection, bringing the realization that theological discourse may only be surface deep because it fails to touch the shared common intellectual stock that lies beneath. Taken together, therefore, these texts form a topology of the mythic dimension of New World experience. Specifically, they do not simply address those realities that form the anatomy of this experience—democracy, machines, political power, and technique—but they address the *meaning* of those realities. Each of the selected texts not only addresses a distinctive feature of the New World topology, but taken together they emanate from generically distinctive regions of thought: epistemology, anthropology, art, and sociology. I believe that if we listen properly, these writers teach us how truly alien are those texts that come to us from the biblical world. It will become evident in the discussion that follows that one thread of thought runs through this topology of the American experience, namely, the problem of time. This is the thread that ultimately binds these texts together and engenders new levels of hermeneutical meaning as we subsequently turn to a reading of the Bible. We may state matters in this way: If technology is the portal of entry to the hermeneutical circle involved with reading the Bible in America, we can further refine matters by recognizing that the problem of time is the portal of entry into understanding technology.

The lingering question is, what have these texts to do with reading the Bible? The "wall of separation" (Thomas Jefferson's phrase) that exists in American culture between church and state demands this question, as do the ecclesiastical theologies of Europe. Yet, is it not precisely Jefferson's wall that must be removed from our intellectual life? It is true that the specialized interests of theology do not reside in the areas of human activity to which these subjects pertain. Who would deny that the intricacies of democratic theory and practice are beyond the purview of theology? Who would argue that it is the work of theology to build a better machine, or make the diverse techniques that run our society more efficient? Yet, at another level, theology has everything to do with these mundane levels of our existence. These enduring realities of American culture are more than simply the key features of our common secular lives; they are the determining elements that shape our entire ethos in both its secular and sacred dimensions. It is because these elements are part and parcel of everything that we are, embedded in everything that we think and read, that they become of primary hermeneutical concern for the public reading of the Bible.

These texts teach us that the most problematical features of our culture are those that are endemic to the very values we advocate most vehemently. It is as America becomes more democratic, in the sense of societal norm given legal sanction, that many of the problems prophetically enunciated by Tocqueville become more pronounced. It is as machines get bigger and more integrated into our environment that the promises of human liberation that they hold become increasingly problematical. It is as the services afforded us by experts in all fields become more and more efficient that we feel increasingly strangled and unable to find our way back to the elemental wellsprings of our lives. What has gone wrong with those salvific implements that were supposed to save us from the common human drudgery that had afflicted all previous societies? Each of these areas seem filled with promises, yet each seems to end in despair—not because the promises are unfulfilled, *but because they have been so completely fulfilled.* Because Americans continue to be increasingly entangled within these instruments of societal salvation that are proclaimed as gospel to the world, these instruments are matters of theological concern. This universal aspect of our cultural ethos raises the concerns of American biblical hermeneutics beyond the regional level to the truly theological one. To whatever degree America is paradigmatic for world civilization, it is a partner in our theological reflection. It is not that our theology ought to become engineering, technocracy, or political science, but only by allowing it to absorb these particular frames of reference might it become more than a superficial activity of the democratic society.

If Tocqueville is correct, the democratic shaping of human experience and perception of the world is the foundation and starting point for all other significant American cultural developments. Democracy lies at the epicenter of the topos of the American experience. Nothing is truly American that stands outside this democratic consciousness, no matter how far evolved from its original conception. Furthermore, the relationship of religion to American democracy is crucial for understanding the dynamics of the democratic experiment in both its sacred and profane dimensions. The specific American brand of democracy that Tocqueville described held religion uniquely in balance with the new freedoms and dangers implicit within the general human drive toward democracy. In his visit to the North American continent, he expressed his admiration for the balanced synthesis of religion and society that appeared to provide for the corrective measures of its own excesses. Yet, in the course of time, he became increasingly suspicious of even the favorable historical accidents of the American experience to hold in check the corroding elements of democracy.

The political and social democracy Tocqueville described and analyzed, however, was a social movement existing in tandem with the broader world of industry and commerce. It was natural that Americans would apply those same democratic principles that guided their collective life to physical and material spheres as well, and that, in so doing, the machine would emerge as the new symbol of a world torn asunder from its traditional values. As Lewis Mumford describes, the machine would embody more than the natural unfolding of democracy into the sphere of nature, because while in the very process of fulfilling democracy, it would bring about the dissolution of the democratic synthesis with the past. The machine became, in the process, imbued with religious qualities—nothing less than a "new messiah," to use Mumford's phrase. The abiding democratic consciousness provided the necessary milieu for the emerging religion. The consequence for traditional religion was fatal. In their inability to adapt to the democratic environment, the traditional religions (predominantly in their European manifestations) continued to play upon the old themes, but found their potency largely sapped by the machine. As a result, those religious images and significations that had beckoned the distinctive American experience in the early period of cultural formation tended to be retained only in an ideological sense, in support of militant America.

The worst fears of Tocqueville and Mumford become an artistic reality in the environment of the Anglo-American totalitarian nightmare sketched out in the political novel *1984* by George Orwell. Totalitarian control of the machine and the means of production bring about an imaginative world entirely bereft of religious institutions and general human spirituality. Here raw political power is viewed as an univocal cultural voice: the marrow of the democratic bone extracted with a precision unknown in Tocqueville's day. And, to round out the picture, just as the Frenchman Tocqueville had seen American democracy in the early nineteenth century as a harbinger of French democracy, so a latter-day Frenchman sees the America of his day as representing "the type that France will represent in thirty years."[2] With the machine as its spearhead, Ellul chronicles the rise of what he terms "technique," an autonomous methodological approach to the world that intends to adapt us more completely to the rationality of the machine: an abstract rationality so finely woven and powerful enough to subsume even the attempts of the state to control it. And, importantly for our theological consideration, rather than allowing a circumscribed place in pluralistic society for the inherited religion[s] of the past as the old democracy had done (even with the advent of the machine), the architects of modern technique prove capable of penetrating the heart of religious life itself and transforming it into another rational instrumentality of the modern world.

Ellul argues that the distinctive features of American ethos are completely subsumed into the universalism of "technique." He distinguishes this ethos only in the sense that it is at the forefront of those cultures involved in the implementation of modern technology. Although it has deeper roots in early Puritan thought, this universalizing trajectory of

---

[2]Jacques Ellul, *The Technological Society* (New York: Alfred A. Knopf, 1976) 117.

American culture was already observed by Tocqueville 150 years ago. It is not the intention of this book to trace this developmental line of thought through the course of American intellectual history. Rather, by beginning with Tocqueville, the discussion is anchored in a watershed text for the quandary of technological America. Already Tocqueville raises the contemporary issues in a formative way that has not been superseded by more recent studies. We may imagine the remaining texts as a kind of chronological commentary on Tocqueville's thesis about the centralizing tendencies of democracy. We are the embodiment of his prophecies.

• The Epistemological Vacuum •

Tocqueville / On the Mythos of the People

Do you wish to raise mankind to an elevated and generous view of the things of this world? Do you want to inspire men with a certain scorn of material goods? Do you hope to engender deep convictions and prepare the way for acts of profound devotion? Are you concerned with refining mores, elevating manners, and causing the arts to blossom? Do you desire poetry, renown, and glory? Do you set out to organize a nation so that it will have a powerful influence over all others? Do you expect it to attempt great enterprises and, whatever be the result of its efforts, to leave a great mark on history? If in your view that should be the main object of men in society, do not support democratic government; it surely will not lead you to that goal.

But if you think it profitable to turn man's intellectual and moral activity toward the necessities of physical life and use them to produce well-being, if you think that reason is more use to men than genius, if your object is not to create heroic virtues but rather tranquil habits, if you would rather contemplate vices than crimes and prefer fewer transgressions at the cost of fewer splendid deeds, if in place of a brilliant society you are content to live in one that is prosperous, and finally, if in your view the main object of government is not to achieve the greatest strength or glory for the nation as a whole but to provide for every individual therein the utmost well-being, protecting him as far as possible from all afflictions, then it is good to make conditions equal and to establish a democratic government.

But if there is not time left to make a choice, and if a force beyond human control is already carrying you along regardless of your desires toward one of these types of government, then at least seek to derive from it all the good that it can do; understanding its good instincts as well as its evil inclinations, try to restrain the latter and promote the former.[3]

Introduction. The French Roman Catholic Alexis de Tocqueville published *Democracy in America* in two parts: the first in 1835 and the second

---

[3]Alexis de Tocqueville, *Democracy in America*, trans. George Lawrence, ed. J. P. Mayer and Max Lerner (New York, Evanston, and London: Harper & Row, 1966) 226.

in 1840. Although significant differences exist in the two parts, I will treat them in my discussion as a whole in accordance with the expressed intention of the author.[4] No book, before or since, has captured the mind of American democracy in a comparable manner to this work. It is fundamental to recognize that the specific variety of democracy investigated by Tocqueville is the American type of the early 1830s; yet, he sees in this phenomenon the fundamental features of all democracies.[5] Nonetheless, he understood this American variety to be distinguishable from those forms that were on the European political horizon by one central feature, namely, here the movement was left "to its own inclinations with hardly any restraint on its instincts."[6] This fact was to be explained historically: "The emigrants who colonized America at the beginning of the seventeenth century in some way separated the principle of democracy from all those other principles against which they contended when living in the heart of the old European societies, and transplanted that principle only on the shores of the New World. It could there grow in freedom and, progressing in conformity with mores, develop peacefully within the law."[7] For Tocqueville, America presented an extracted form of pure democracy and was, therefore, a fascinating laboratory in which certain extremist mistakes could be weeded out before its full implementation on

---

[4]In a note to himself on 5 February 1838, Tocqueville wrote, "I have been led in the second work to take up once more subjects already handled in the first, or to modify some opinions expressed there, a necessary result of so large a work done in two parts"; in Yale Tocqueville-Beaumont MSS C.V. k. (copy of notes for the *Démocratie* of 1840) packet 7, notebook 1, page 50. Quoted in Seymour Drescher, "Tocqueville's Two *Démocraties*," in *Journal of the History of Ideas* 15:2 (April–June 1964): 202.

[5]Concerning the second part of his work, Tocqueville wrote in a letter to John Stuart Mill in 1840: "When I wrote only of the democratic society in the United States, I was quickly understood. If I had spoken of our democratic society in France as it appears at present it would be even more easily grasped. But starting from ideas given me by American and French society I wanted to paint the general features of democratic societies of which no complete specimen yet exists. This is where I lose the ordinary reader. Only those very used to the search for general and speculative truths care to follow me in such a direction. I think that it is due to the original sin of the subject, rather than to the way in which I treated any portion of it that I must attribute the comparatively weaker effect produced by this work." Quoted by Drescher, "Two *Démocraties*," 201; cf. Alexis de Tocqueville, *Correspondance Anglaise: Correspondance d'Alesis de Tocqueville avec Henry Reeve et John Stuart Mill*, vol. 6 of *Oeuvres complètes*, definitive edition published under the direction of J. P. Mayer (Paris: Gallimard, 1954) 330 (Tocqueville to Mill, 18 December 1840).

[6]Tocqueville, *Democracy in America*, 12.

[7]Ibid., 11.

French soil. The America that Tocqueville visited was the one of popular Jacksonian democracy. Playing the part of the astute outsider, Tocqueville himself was able to capture artistically the virgin democratic spirit that was superseding Jeffersonian America with a freshness, originality, and profundity reserved for those present during early creative periods. His study of democracy penetrates as deeply today as when it was first written, one of those rare analyses whose worth and value seems to increase rather than diminish with age.

John Stuart Mill very quickly captured the power of Tocqueville's achievement when he wrote, "[*Democracy in America* is] the first philosophical book ever written on democracy as it manifests itself in modern society; a book, the essential doctrines of which it is not likely that any future speculations will subvert, to whatever degree they may modify them."[8] Although authored by a trained lawyer, it is this deeply philosophical nature of the text of *Democracy in America* that carries the reader to the core of the democratic mind. Much of the religious life and thought of American civilization lies embedded in the democratic substratum of the culture that Tocqueville lays bare. Since my task is to bring about a better understanding of the effect of that culture on the way we read the Bible, Tocqueville's monumental work stands as a resource of prime importance.

The Tyranny of the People. Tocqueville begins his study of American democracy with the following statement, "No novelty in the United States struck me more vividly during my stay there than the equality of conditions." He continues, "I soon realized that the influence of this fact extends far beyond political mores and laws, exercising dominion over civil society as much as over the government; it creates opinions, gives birth to feelings, suggests customs, and modifies whatever it does not create. So the more I studied American society, the more clearly I saw equality of conditions as the creative element from which each particular fact derived, and all my observations constantly returned to this nodal point."[9] This pervasive equality of life that formed the "nodal point" of American life was not an unmitigated blessing, and the remainder of *Democracy in America* is a detailed examination of its negative, as well as its positive, ramifications. Democracy itself was inevitable; but its potentially debilitative effects were not. Thus, while Tocqueville was an aristocrat, and his point of reference for analyzing democracy was set in this older worldview, one should not take his criticisms of democratic man as absolute. In fact, because he argued that democracy was indeed capable of reform, he should be classified as a genuine friend and advocate of it. Rather than hold Tocqueville's aristocratic roots as an indication of his inability to fully accept the new ways, I would argue that it was to his benefit to be solidly

---

[8]Ibid., xii.

[9]Ibid., 3.

grounded in a cultural system different from the one that he chose to analyze. This very fact, coupled with his obvious sensitivities, allowed him to penetrate intellectually far more deeply than would otherwise have been the case. Importantly, for example, Tocqueville did not argue that the centralized power of the older European aristocracies was superior to the decentralized democracy of America. In fact, just the opposite was the case: it was the potential development of centralized power in the new democracy itself that was to be guarded against. His penetrating look at the heart of democracy revealed the paradox of a people free on the surface, but internally yearning for and gravitating toward centralized political power as a compensation for the responsibilities and risks of liberty.

> Since in times of equality no man is obliged to put his powers at the disposal of another, and no one has any claim or right to substantial support from his fellow man, each is both independent and weak. These two conditions, which must be neither seen quite separately nor confused, give the citizen of a democracy extremely contradictory instincts. He is full of confidence and pride in his independence among his equals, but from time to time his weakness makes him feel the need for some outside help which he cannot expect from any of his fellows, for they are both impotent and cold. In this extremity he naturally turns his eyes toward that huge entity which alone stands out above the universal level of abasement. His needs, and even more his longings, continually put him in mind of that entity, and he ends by regarding it as the sole and necessary support of his individual weakness.[10]

For Tocqueville, therefore, political systems should not be seen in abstraction. While they frame certain vital areas of human activity, they are always embodied in the complexities of human existence and are thus subject to the weaknesses of the flesh. Since democracy exists in the midst of a more broadly based civilization, he argues forcefully for its examination in this wider context.

This tendency of a free people seeking after centralized power represents the fundamental tension of democracy, and its redress was Tocqueville's fundamental intention in writing the book.[11] His own footnote to the above text is as prophetic as it is powerful.

> In democratic societies the central power alone has both some stability and some capacity to see its undertakings through. All the citizenry is ever moving and changing around. Now, it is in the nature of every government to wish continually to increase its sphere of action. Moreover, it is almost bound ultimately to succeed in this, for it acts with fixed purpose and determination on men whose position, ideas, and desires change every

---

[10]Ibid., 648.

[11]"I am certainly not the one to say that such inclinations are invincible, for my chief aim in writing this book is to combat them." Cf. ibid., 647.

day. *Often the citizens, without intending to, play into its hands* [my emphasis].[12]

In this way, Tocqueville saw the freedoms that accompanied democracy as leaving a stability vacuum in society that only a centralized government could fill. Freedom, it seemed to him, existed in symbiotic relationship with power. This insight set the context for his dire prospect for democracy enunciated in 1840.

> I believe that it is easier to establish an absolute and despotic government among a people whose social conditions are equal than among any other. I also believe that such a government once established in such a people would not only oppress men but would, in the end, strip each man there of several of the chief attributes of humanity.
> *I therefore think that despotism is particularly to be feared in ages of democracy* [my emphasis].[13]

For him, by the time he wrote the second volume of *Democracy in America* in 1840, democracy and political tyranny had come to be almost synonymous. The public centrality of power has a way of rising to the surface in democratic times, regardless of institutional safeguards designed to keep it at bay.

How do the citizens, keen on their own individual freedom, play into the hands of an ever more centralized government? They make the mistake of requesting the assistance of the state in their own private affairs while working to restrict it in all others. Time is therefore on the side of the state: "the simple fact of its continuing existence increases the attributes of power of a democratic government. . . . the passions of individuals, in spite of themselves, promote it; and one can say that the older a democratic society, the more centralized will its government be."[14] The fundamental insight at this revealing point in the book is that Tocqueville saw democracy as unable to eradicate those basic problems of human existence that are not grounded in a rational form of government but are grounded in the passions. Indeed, as he makes clear continually throughout the book, democracy actually fosters and nurtures those very passions, such as greed, pride, and self-pleasure, which work against the very freedoms that the democratic system itself promotes. Democracy, in short, runs its course in a vicious circle that feeds upon itself. The pressing need, therefore, that Tocqueville explicitly gives reference is as follows: "The first duty imposed on those who now direct society is to educate democracy; to put, if possible, new life into its beliefs; to purify its mores; to control its actions; gradually to substitute understanding of

---

[12]Ibid., 648.

[13]Ibid., 670.

[14]Ibid., 648.

statecraft for present inexperience and knowledge of its true interests for blind instincts; to adapt government to the needs of time and place; and to modify it as men and circumstances require."[15] The intention of Tocqueville's literary work is to educate and uplift the moral life of the democratic nation. Religion is viewed as a part of this necessarily ongoing process, as is, for example, the study of the classics. And, there is no indication that Tocqueville expects the task to be easily completed or quickly done. The power of this work stems from this dynamic focus.

Such texts as noted above help the reader penetrate the deepest layers of Tocqueville's work and reveal that quality that makes it a classic of our civilization. The focus of *Democracy in America* is not simply on the past, present, or future of democratic society. It is on all three of these at once, and it intends to bring to the reader an immediate encounter with the mind of democracy. It is this sense of immediacy that makes the work a classic and gives it an extraordinary power of conviction. Similar to the Bible, the intent is prescriptive, rather than descriptive. The book has a long-term mission to perform, and it is this sense of mission that carries it from generation to generation. In hermeneutical fashion, Tocqueville retrieves certain categories from the old aristocratic worldview that he believes have been too hastily bypassed in the new democratic age and applies them in his diagnosis of its present-day failures. His analysis is directed to one overriding reality that he found in the New World: "It is safe to foresee that trust in common opinion will become a sort of religion, with the majority as its prophet."[16] But his is not a simple apologetic for the values of a bygone era advocating the return to an aristocratic form of government. He presupposed that democracy had become a fact of life in America, and would soon become so in France. Tocqueville is sensitive to those aspects of democracy that have the potential of ultimately increasing, rather than decreasing, human suffering by means of the uncritical acceptance of a growing centralized government: "I am certainly not the one to say that such inclinations are invincible, for my chief aim in writing this book is to combat them."[17] The work is, therefore, optimistic in its pessimistic voice.

The advent of the age of equality, therefore, represented a dual-edged sword: the very opportunities that it presented society offered avenues of tyranny unknown even in aristocratic times. It is especially in the second part of *Democracy in America*, during the period of further reflection on his experience of America and the intervening events, that Tocqueville increasingly came to envision concentrated public power as the

---

[15]Ibid., 6.

[16]Ibid., 400.

[17]Ibid., 647.

nemesis of democratic governments.[18] Near the end of the book, Tocqueville concludes, "I believe that it is easier to establish an absolute and despotic government among a people whose social conditions are equal than among any other."[19] His warning is uncategorical: "I therefore think that despotism is particularly to be feared in ages of democracy."[20] Despotism can enter into human community through two fundamental tendencies produced by a society of social equality: "one turns each man's attention to new thoughts, while the other would induce him freely to give up thinking at all."[21] Tyranny is an old human foe, only its guise has become more subtle in a democratic system.[22] Tyranny arises in democracy because "the absolute sovereignty of the will of the majority is the essence

---

[18]Drescher, "Two *Démocraties*," describes Tocqueville's evolving view in this way:

> In the final chapters of the 1840 study centralization almost superseded *démocratie* as the providential end toward which all humanity was moving. No longer historically inert like those societies with which it was first identified, it had become the frankenstein of the egalitarian process. . . . The *Démocratie* of 1840 . . . emphasized the increasing power of the magistracy in spite of the instability of the magistrates. It had become the heir of the democratic revolution, like the aristocracy of 1835, a body which never dies. Not the elected magistrate but the eternal ministerial hierarchy was the focus of attention; not the multiplicity of electoral and revolutionary changes, but the institution which seemed to benefit by all revolutions. The ruler was no longer only a man momentarily thrust into power to be swept away with the next shift in the mood of the people, but the ubiquitous and omnipotent state itself. (213)

[19]Tocqueville, *Democracy in America*, 670.

[20]Ibid., 670. He continues, "I think that at all times I should have loved freedom, but in the times in which we live, I am disposed to worship it." However, there is "no question of reconstructing an aristocratic society, but the need is to make freedom spring from that democratic society in which God has placed us."

[21]Ibid., 401.

[22]Tocqueville was less than sanguine about the results of the French Revolution, which he saw as the model of those *not* inspired by freedom. Irene Coltman Brown notes, "Inevitably, it appeared, these revolutions erupted with great violence but ended with a reassertion of a single or central authority before which all men were equal in their loss of freedom but which they passively accepted because, through the long experience of futile revolutionary violence, the revolutionaries themselves had come to feel contempt for their own convictions. 'When people assert that nothing is safe from revolutions,' said Tocqueville, 'I tell them they are wrong, and that centralisation is one of those things. How could it ever perish? The enemies of government love it and those who govern cherish it.' " In Brown, "Tocqueville, Democracy & Revolution," *History Today* 31 (September 1981): 31.

of democratic government, for in democracies there is nothing outside the majority capable of resisting it."[23] Democracy at its most fundamental level, therefore, is the rule of the majority over the minority.[24] This majority does not rule in its own name, but in the name of the people: "until our day it had been thought that despotism was odious, whatever form it took. But now it has been discovered that there are legitimate tyrannies in this world and holy injustices, provided that it is all done in the people's name."[25] Only education could act as a safeguard against this new tyranny of the majority: the sort of guidance that Tocqueville's book is clearly intended to provide. In order to better understand this intention, it is essential to penetrate to the core of his philosophy.

The Escape to the New and the Quick. Tocqueville argues that "the people" was only the newest of intellectual abstractions by which oppression and inhumanity might be imposed. The people's democracy was even more dangerous than the aristocratic institutions it replaced because, while its violent acts were intellectual, this very fact made them more incisive than aristocratic tyrannies.

> Princes made violence a physical thing, but our contemporary democratic republics have turned it into something as intellectual as the human will it is intended to constrain. Under the absolute government of a single man, despotism, to reach the soul, clumsily struck at the body, and the soul, escaping from such blows, rose gloriously above it; but in democratic republics that is not at all how tyranny behaves; *it leaves the body alone and goes straight for the soul* [my emphasis].[26]

Tocqueville consistently maintained that democracy changed the ground rules of *every* aspect of life. In that sense, it was more than simply a political experience, it was a spiritual one. It was because of its all-encompassing nature that democracy commanded the attention of religion. It remained for the theoretical mind to think through the implications of this "spiritual conversion" that was transforming the world. In the second volume of his original work, Tocqueville specifically delineated those major aspects of American life upon which the experience of the people's democracy was having a profound effect, namely, its intellectual movements, sentiments, mores, and political life. Above all else, Tocqueville's massive study is an attempt to lay bare the fundamental effect of American democratic experience and the other personal and communal consequences that flowed from it. It is important for this study of Amer-

---

[23]Tocqueville, *Democracy in America*, 227.

[24]In this system, for example, the police "are nothing but the majority under arms." Ibid., 233.

[25]Ibid., 363.

[26]Ibid., 236.

ican biblical hermeneutics to set forth the major features of this issue.

Tocqueville begins the second volume of *Democracy in America* with four important chapters that describe in some detail the effect of democracy on the way Americans think.[27] Quite appropriately, religious themes are woven through these chapters as well. A basic grasp of these ideas is fundamental to understanding his portrayal of the democratic experience, and the role that religion might play in it. While noting that Americans are unconcerned and ignorant of rival European schools of philosophy, he nevertheless observes that "it is noticeable that the people of the United States almost all have a uniform method and rules for the conduct of intellectual inquiries."[28] Because of this nonreflective aspect of the American character, it remained for the scholar to flesh out the fundamentals of its thinking process. This he does briefly as follows.

> To escape from imposed systems, the yoke of habit, family maxims, class prejudices, and a certain extent national prejudices as well; to treat tradition as valuable for information only and to accept existing facts as no more than a useful sketch to show how things could be done differently and better; to seek by themselves and in themselves for the only reason for things, looking to results without getting entangled in the means toward them and looking through forms to the basis of things—such are the principal characteristics of what I would call the American philosophical method. To carry the argument further and to select the chief among these various features, and the one which includes almost all the others within itself, I should say that in most mental operations each American relies on individual effort and judgment. So, of all countries in the world, America is the one in which the precepts of Descartes are least studied and best followed.[29]

In this way Tocqueville sees the effects of democratic individualism as determining intellectual and spiritual existence, as well as social and political life. We may isolate the fundamental features of the American intellect as follows.

1. It is based on *individual* effort and judgment.
2. It is based on *escape* from those aspects of the past that impede individual freedom.
3. It *transforms* tradition into something useful.
4. It is *result-oriented*, rather than means-oriented.
5. It is interested in *substance* rather than form.
6. It is *Cartesian* in outlook.

I would maintain that these points do indeed form an excellent matrix of characteristics of the American mind, and that they hold the highest im-

---

[27]Ibid., 393–407.

[28]Ibid., 393.

[29]Ibid., 393.

plications for understanding the way we read the Bible in our culture, a matter to which we shall return below. Furthermore, I would summarize many of these intellectual characteristics as at least incipiently technological in orientation in the sense that they are future- and goal-oriented. The cumulative effect of all these characteristics of democratic thought is a devastating attack upon the pull of *pastness*. Clearly, the desire to escape from the geography of the Old World to the New implied the corollary of escape from the old (aristocratic) ways of thinking as well.

The pull of the new and unexamined in intellectual matters means that Americans free themselves at one level of human existence, only to fall victim to the uncritical sway of ideas at another. No person can live perpetually in the vacuum of individualism; just as no person can live perpetually on the run from the past. In Tocqueville's perceptive analysis, the American mind is geared toward both. It is a false metaphysics that distorts all other thought processes. The problem becomes one of coming to terms honestly with the fresh opportunities and dangers of the American experience, while not using that experience as a means of evading the universal problems of human existence. Upon our ability to make this fine, but clear, demarcation, rests the potential of American thought. The particular danger of democratic thinking of which Tocqueville warns is its susceptibility to taking the opinions of others "on trust without discussion," that is, as dogma. Dogma is particularly appealing in an open and free environment, because no mind can engage everything and live in a state of "perpetual excitement." The result is that it is illusory to think that democracy will lead people away from authority: "Somewhere and somehow authority is always bound to play a part in intellectual and moral life. . . . The independence of the individual may be greater or less but can never be unlimited. *Therefore we need not inquire about the existence of intellectual authority in democratic ages, but only where it resides and what its limits are*" [my emphasis].[30] Therefore, at best, intellectual freedom in a democratic society is relative and limited. The danger is that it will be taken as an absolute.

It is perhaps the intoxication of the promise of freedom that causes the democratic citizen to yearn for it to a degree that is de facto unattainable. And, in this instance when reality denies the intellectual prize for which the social structure is so primed and ready to achieve, the placebo of public opinion is offered instead. Tocqueville writes, "The nearer men are to a common level of uniformity, the less are they inclined to believe blindly in any man or any class. But they are readier to trust the mass, and public

---

[30]Ibid., 399.

opinion becomes more and more mistress of the world."[31] In this way, the achievement of equality in society seduces the citizenry into a false belief in the equality of truth; that is, that truth, left unheeded, will reveal itself to the greatest number. It is the final step in the democratic process of quantification (the determination of truth by the majority), and has significant religious ramifications. Tocqueville continues, "The intellectual dominion of the greatest number . . . will always be very nearly absolute in times of equality."[32] I take this statement to be a profound insight into the precondition of democratic mentality before democratic polity. The significance of this book is largely tied up with Tocqueville's recognition of this fact, and his exploitation of it. It is to be expected that his work is often ignored by the majority today who are bound to the very dogmatic ways of thinking to which he was pointing.

Dogmatism is bound up with another characteristic of democratic thinking that lies at the very heart of its thought processes: the tendency to think in general ideas.[33] Tocqueville unequivocally condemns this intellectual tendency in American society by anchoring his criticism of it in religion.

> The Deity does not view the human race collectively. With one glance He sees every human being separately and sees in each the resemblances that make him like his fellows and the differences which isolate him from them.
> It follows that God has no need of general ideas, that is to say, He never feels the necessity of giving the same label to a considerable number of analogous objects in order to think about them more conveniently.
> It is not like that with man.[34]

Whatever other differences one wishes to maintain, Tocqueville argues that the human mind differs from the divine in the one specific sense of this need for "convenience." Humans must resort to general ideas because of the necessity of transcending the details of life in order to arrive at larger fields of meaning. God, on the other hand, has the ability to arrive at larger units of meaning without resorting to generalization. Un-

---

[31]Ibid. He continues, "In times of equality men, being so like each other, have no confidence in others, but this same likeness leads them to place almost unlimited confidence in the judgment of the public, for they think it not unreasonable that, all having the same means of knowledge, truth will be found on the side of the majority" (p. 400).

[32]Ibid., 400.

[33]The most important place that this is discussed is vol. 2, pt. 1, chap. 3: "Why the Americans Show More Aptitude and Taste for General Ideas Than Their English Forefathers," 402–405.

[34]Ibid., 402.

fortunately, the human need for generalization brings as many woes to intellectual matters as it brings benefits: "General ideas have this excellent quality, that they permit human minds to pass judgment quickly on a great number of things; but the conceptions they convey are always incomplete, and what is gained in extent is always lost in exactitude." In this way, Tocqueville perceives that generalizations do not allow us to think better, only quicker. The power of generalized thinking necessarily incorporated throughout the range of intellectual activity represents a speeding up of the everyday uses to which we put the mind. Presumably, given enough time (and brain capacity), humans could work through the details of life one by one in a way analogous to God's method. But such a situation is unimaginable. The price humans pay for this sort of poor imitation of divine thinking is approximation and inexactitude. And it was precisely these sorts of intellectual characteristics that Tocqueville viewed in unprecedented abundance during his American visit.

What was it about the American democratic experience that caused generalized thinking to flourish? The answer is rooted in those same democratic traits of society to which Tocqueville refers throughout his book: equality and individualism.

> I have shown before how equal standards induce each man to look for truth for himself. It is easy to see that such a method insensibly directs the human spirit toward generalizations. When traditions of class, of profession, and of family are repudiated and the dominion of precedent is left behind for the search by one's own unaided reason for the way to follow, one has a natural inclination to deduce the motives for one's views from the very nature of man, and that leads of necessity and almost in spite of oneself to a great number of very broad generalizations.[35]

The democratic tendency of sweeping away all traditional aids for the tasks of thinking has resulted in an over reliance upon reason itself. This naked reason carries with it the seeds of destruction due to its increased reliance upon its power of generalization. The more the demands, the more the dependence upon general ideas with their lessened capacity to see the fine details of reality upon which general ideas must be based.[36] Coupled with the heightened tendency for success and pleasure that individualism brings, this means that democratic citizens "want great success at once, but they want to do without great efforts." Therefore, it is in this vein that Tocqueville concludes with this picture of democratic men.

> These contrary instincts lead them straight to looking for generalizations, by means of which they flatter themselves that they can paint vast

---

[35]Ibid., 404.

[36]At one point Tocqueville remarks, "Nothing is so unproductive for the human mind as an abstract idea." Cf. ibid., 593.

canvases very cheaply and attract public attention without trouble.

I do not know that they are wrong in thinking so. For their readers are just as afraid of profundity as they are themselves and generally look only for facile pleasures and effortless instruction in the works of the mind.[37]

Generalization feeds upon generalization, and inaccuracy builds upon inaccuracy. Fine nuances are passed over by the democratic mind that is in a hurry to achieve greatness without the accompanying willingness to spend the necessary time in the details that lay the foundation for greatness. It is a dire prospect for the life of the mind in America!

An additional reason for the American tendency to generalize ideas is rooted in the effects of the life-style it engenders. Tocqueville maintains that the only effective way to combat the terrors of general conception is to force a continual interaction or dialogue of these general conceptions with reality. The problem at this point is the old nemesis of time: "Citizens of democracies are greedy for general ideas because they have little leisure, and such conceptions save them from wasting time considering particular cases."[38] However, while Americans do not have (or take) the time to examine closely the general concepts of "mercantile theory, politics, science, and the arts," general concepts in the case of the two former areas are accepted by Americans only after examination "and even then they do so with reserve." He concludes, "That is how democratic institutions which make each citizen take a practical part in government moderate the excessive taste for general political theories which is prompted by equality." In light of the fact that Tocqueville sees the essential fabric of the American mind as being antitheoretical at its central core, he seems to leave open the probability that the same sort of structure of activity is true for American religious life as well.

Religion in Negative Dialectic to Democracy. Liberal biblical scholarship argues for the progressive intellectual and social implications of religion in the broader cultural context. For Tocqueville, several important distinctions need to be made in terms of such issues. It is fallacious to dismiss his point of view as attributable to an aristocratic background. Something of enduring value lies embedded in his approach to this subject. By way of background, he does nothing to hide his partisanship to Roman Catholicism. He categorized the American taste for "enthusiastic forms of spirituality" as "religious madness." He writes, "Although the desire to acquire the good things of this world is the dominant passion among Americans, there are momentary respites when their souls seem suddenly to break the restraining bonds of matter and rush impetuously heavenward."[39] We see here that the key to understanding much of the

---

[37]Ibid., 405.

[38]Ibid., 406.

[39]Ibid., 506. In general, see 506–507 for Tocqueville's discussion of this subject.

American religious experience begins by taking into account the under-lying, overwhelming materialism of its culture. God had implanted in humans the taste for the infinite and immortal. Therefore, "the soul has needs which must be satisfied. Whatever pains are taken to distract it from itself, it soon grows bored, restless, and anxious amid the pleasures of the sense." Furthermore, Tocqueville speculates that "if ever the thoughts of the great majority of mankind came to be concentrated solely on the search for material blessings, one can anticipate that there would be a co-lossal reaction in the souls of men. They would distractedly launch out into the world of spirits for fear of being held too tightly bound by the body's fetters." In this way, materialism and spirituality are seen to be locked in a sort of inverted relationship to one another. When one flour-ishes, the other wanes. In America, with its crass materialism and pro-motion of individual human desires, it is inevitable that such distortions would cause its spiritual life to exceed the limits of common sense. In such a situation, Tocqueville saw his own Roman Catholic tradition making its most valuable contribution to American democratic life by drawing upon its aristocratic roots in European culture. This represented a contribution that was fundamentally at odds with the new American democratic so-ciety in which it operated.

In order for genuine religious life to make a valued contribution to so-ciety, a certain aloofness from it had to be maintained. In Tocqueville's terms,

> The greatest advantage of religions is to inspire diametrically contrary urges. Every religion places the object of man's desires outside and be-yond worldly goods and naturally lifts the soul into regions far above the realm of the senses. Every religion also imposes on each man some obli-gations toward mankind, to be performed in common with the rest of mankind, and so draws him away, from time to time, from thinking about himself. That is true even of the most false and dangerous religions.
> *Thus religious peoples are naturally strong just at the point where democratic peoples are weak.* And that shows how important it is for people to keep their religion when they become equal [author's emphasis].[40]

Here Tocqueville makes the point that the greatest strength of religion is its own internal dialectic between worldliness (morality) and otherworld-liness (dogma). Thus, whereas democracy draws people in upon them-selves, emphasizing individual achievement and self-aggrandizement, religion focuses the mind away from the self "outside and beyond worldly goods" and the senses. It is in this sense that he can characterize religion in general, and Christianity in particular, as being diametrically opposed to democracy. It is not an opposition based on political theory but one based on duality of purpose. The fact that religion is bipolar within itself

---

[40]Ibid., 410.

means that it *cannot* identify fully with any particular worldly (political) philosophy. This does not imply that religion ought to oppose a democratic form of government; rather, it is to acknowledge that authentic religion and democracy are not the same. Tocqueville saw the distorted forms of "enthusiastic spirituality" that populated the American landscape as the result of the symbiotic relationship between religion and democracy. All too frequently in American life, religion had lost its own integrity and had become an appendage of the democratic society. Therefore, religion ought to be unequivocal and dogmatic in terms of its answers to the primordial questions of life as a guard against democratic usurpation.

Tocqueville's defense of aristocratic and dogmatic religion must be set in his own historical and cultural context in order to transcend its negative implications. While it may be true that in order to maintain its vitality in a democratic time such as our own, religion must be more attuned to the democratic experience than he allows, especially problematic is his refusal to rethink the fundamental (primordial) teachings of religion in light of the new experience. At this point, he himself falls victim to the very Cartesian dualism he otherwise criticizes. He clearly understands religion as being an independent reality that properly brings some*thing* to the democratic experience in terms of being a corrective force. The primary example that he draws upon at the core of the American experience is New England Puritanism.

> In New England, where education and liberty spring from morality and religion and where an already old and long-settled society has been able to shape its own maxims and habits, the people, though rid of all forms of superiority ever created by wealth or birth among men, are accustomed to respect intellectual and moral superiority and to submit thereto without displeasure; and so we find New England democracy making choices better than those made elsewhere.[41]

New England democracy is the example of what all of American democracy might have been: a political system built upon the teachings of morality and religion. The development and nurture of these teachings make a viable democracy possible—one that maintains the values of virtue and excellence rooted in aristocratic social structures.

This viewpoint is corroborated by the single fact of history that of all immigrants to the New World, only the New Englanders came for an *idea*.[42] All others had come to better their position or accumulate wealth, and not for an "intellectual craving." The contrast with the remainder of America was sharp: "But as one goes farther south to those states where

---

[41]Ibid., 185.

[42]Ibid., 30.

the social tie is less old and less strong, where education is less wide-spread, and where principles of morality, religion, and liberty are less happily combined, one finds both talents and virtues becoming rarer among those in authority."[43] Thus, the type of democracy that was to prevail in America was a sort of untamed, independent one that had broken too strictly from the aristocratic past. Religion and education were the fundamental activities that might serve as a bridge to the past, as the institutional means whereby the past might retain its voice in the present.[44] Such a role necessitates an independence from the prevailing cultural winds and the retention of certain features of the old dogmatic ways of aristocratic society as a defense against the onslaught of democracy, which pits itself against those values of the aristocratic past that need to be maintained as a way of taming and civilizing it. Therefore, it was not the aristocratic past that Tocqueville was defending, it was rather more the idea of pastness *as such*. He believed that democracies were particularly weak at this point of the neglect of pastness, and that the particular facilities of those engaged in religion and education in utilizing the past was precisely the antidote that was needed in the new world that was emerging. As a result, Tocqueville implies that in the context of the democratic assault on time in which it tends to be robbed of its futurity in the passions and desires of the present, religion has a retarding role to play by keeping alive the past realities operative in present experience.

A major issue that Tocqueville's analysis of the role of traditional religion in democratic society raises is the one of the relation of church and state. He is clear that religion ought to be established independent of the state. In this regard he writes,

> So long as a religion derives its strength from sentiments, instincts, and passions, which are reborn in like fashion in all periods of history, it can

---

[43]Ibid., 185.

[44]In terms of education, Tocqueville makes the following points in his discussion of classical literature in vol. 2, pt. 1, chap. 15 ("Why the Study of Greek and Latin Literature Is Peculiarly Useful in Democratic Societies"), pp. 444-45:

> No other literature puts in bolder relief just those qualities democratic writers tend to lack, and therefore no other literature is better to be studied at such time. . . . An obstinate determination to teach nothing but the classics in a society always struggling to acquire or keep wealth would produce very well-educated but very dangerous citizens. For the state of politics and society would always make them want things which their education had not taught them how to earn, and they would perturb the state, in the name of the Greeks and Romans, instead of enriching it by their industry. . . . Not that I hold the classics beyond criticism, but I think that they have special merits well calculated to counterbalance our peculiar defects. They provide a prop just where we are most likely to fall.

brave the assaults of time, or at least it can only be destroyed by another religion. But when a religion chooses to rely on the interests of this world, it becomes almost as fragile as all earthly powers. Alone, it may hope for immortality; linked to ephemeral powers, it follows their fortunes and often falls together with the passions of a day sustaining them.

Hence any alliance with any political power whatsoever is bound to be burdensome for religion. It does not need their support in order to live, and in serving them it may die.[45]

This comment, and others, makes clear Tocqueville's perspective: the separation of church and state in America is a good thing because it creates a beneficial partnership for religion as well as the state.[46] Too close an alliance with the state means that religion will suffer similar ravages of historical vicissitude. Only outright independence will serve to protect religion. Religion should be, we might say, above it all. Yet, this very independence of religion in democratic society means that two new dangers appear on the horizon: schism and indifference. Rather than an unholy alliance with the state, the problem now is that

a religious belief is silently undermined by doctrines which I shall call negative because they assert the falseness of one religion but do not establish the truth of any other.

Then vast revolutions take place in the human mind without the apparent cooperation of the passions of man and almost without his knowledge [my emphasis]. One sees some men lose, as from forgetfulness, the object of their dearest hopes. Carried away by an imperceptible current against which they have not the courage to struggle but to which they yield with regret, they abandon the faith they love to follow the doubt that leads them to despair.

In such ages beliefs are forsaken through indifference rather than from hate; without being rejected, they fall away.[47]

This "silent revolution" of democracy is a further unfolding of the violence that is directed toward the intellect that I discussed above. It is far less visible than open hostility, but ultimately at least as effective. The very passions that democratic individualism unleashes work contrary to religion. "With unbelievers hiding their incredulity and believers avowing

---

[45]Ibid., 274.

[46]George Armstrong Kelly makes the following observation: "Tocqueville felt that the democratic and irreligious impulses had formed an unwholesome alliance in France. He was thus reassured to discover religion and the new era of the common man in partnership in America. He did not ask religion to perform saintly wonders, nor did he demand Roman virtue from the politics of the coming age. His goal was a moderate 'harmonization.' " In "Faith, Freedom, and Disenchantment: Politics and the American Religious Consciousness," *Daedalus* 3:1 (Winter 1982): 135.

[47]Tocqueville, *Democracy in America*, 275.

their faith, a public opinion favorable to religion takes shape; religion is loved, supported, and honored, and only by looking into the depths of men's souls will one see what wounds it has suffered."[48] In this way, Tocqueville argues that religious matters have become more complex in a raw democratic society. Separation of church and state has saved the church from the political intrigues of Europe, only to cause it to fall victim to a new set of enemies. He gives us little concrete hope that the theology that is generated by democratic society is equal to the task of coming to terms with these new challenges. How will religion retain its vitality in light of this cultural indifference that is gnawing away at it from the inside? How can its theologians be immune to the same tyranny of the intellect that affects all members of the egalitarian society? What will stop religion from being smothered by the kindnesses and accolades that precede indifference? Has the separation of church and state merely postponed the inevitable?

• Anthropological, Political, and Sociological Critiques •

Mumford / On Machines as Anthropological Messianism

Through the more conscious cultivation of the machine arts and through greater selectivity in their use, one sees the pledge of its wider fulfillment throughout civilization. For at the bottom of that cultivation there must be the direct and immediate experience of living itself: we must directly see, feel, touch, manipulate, sing, dance, communicate before we can extract from the machine any further sustenance for life. If we are empty to begin with, the machine will only leave us emptier; if we are passive and powerless to begin with, the machine will only leave us more feeble.[49]

Introduction. The move from democracy to technology is a natural one to make in the description of the interior landscape of New World mythos. Democracy and modern technology stand in the closest of symbiotic relationships: Democracy is the application of modern technological principles to government, whereas, modern technology is the application of democratic theory to matter. A decade ago, C. B. Macpherson further refined the relationship in this way:

> The ontological assumptions of our Western democratic theory [comprise] two concepts of the human essence. One of these is the liberal, individualist concept of man as essentially a consumer of utilities, an infinite desirer and infinite appropriator. This concept antedates the introduction of democratic principles. The other is the concept of man as an enjoyer and exerter of his uniquely human attributes or capacities, a view that began

---

[48]Ibid., 276.

[49]Lewis Mumford, *Technics and Civilization* (New York: Harcourt, Brace & World, 1963) 344.

to challenge the market view in the mid-nineteenth century and soon became an integral part of the justifying theory of liberal democracy.[50]

Both of these understandings of humanity remain central to the American dream in our own day. Set in the context of historic philosophy and theology, they represent radical reformulations of the meaning of human existence. If we add the influence of the mentality of technological experimentation on the establishment and course of American democracy, the ties between the two are seen all the more strongly.[51] In this context, it is instructive to turn to an analysis of the interior meaning of the artifact that would be the harbinger of technological prosperity in the democratic republic: the machine.

In 1934, with the publication of *Technics and Civilization*, Lewis Mumford offered the first American attempt to give an exhaustive account of the meaning of the machine that had arisen to a position of such dominance throughout Western civilization. His examination of the effect of machines on all of society crisscrossed the artificial boundaries of academic disciplines, and has remained a classic study of this subject, which he identified as "technics."[52] Clearly, this work goes beyond the specific study of American society as such.[53] As Alan Trachtenberg has recently pointed out, with the publication of *The Brown Decades: A Study of the Arts in America, 1865–1895* in 1931, Mumford had completed nearly a decade

---

[50]C. B. Macpherson, "Democratic Theory: Ontology and Technology," in Carl Mitcham and Robert Mackey, eds., *Philosophy and Technology* (New York: Macmillan, 1983) 161.

[51]Daniel Boorstin writes, "When we look back on the series of events between 1776 and 1789 which brought forth the United States of America, we must first be struck that the leaders were interested less in the ideology—the formulation of a systematic philosophy—than in the technology of politics. They were testing well-known principles by applying them to their specific problems. Their special concern was 'to organize the means for satisfying needs and desires'—which is a dictionary definition of technology. There are a number of clues to this open, experimental, *technological* spirit of our North American revolutionaries." Cf. *The Republic of Technology* (New York: Harper & Row, 1978) 49.

[52]Mumford's work on time is taken up and developed, for example, in David S. Landes, *Revolution in Time: Clocks and the Making of the Modern World* (Cambridge MA and London: Harvard University Press, 1983) esp. ch. 4.

[53]Eddy Dow makes the point that the period between *The Brown Decades* (1931) and *Technics and Civilization* (1934) represented "the most important shift in his career." That was because "Mumford enlarged both the source of the materials for his synthesis and the context in which those materials are interpreted from American to Western and, latterly, to world civilization." Cf. Dow, "Lewis Mumford's Passage to India: From the First to the Later Phase," *South Atlantic Quarterly* 76:1 (Winter 1977): 33–34.

of work specifically devoted to American studies.[54] It is important to understand, however, that his carefully crafted career as a writer was self-consciously constructed in such a way that his early work on American culture was subsequently expanded into the broader contexts of Western and world civilization, rather than being displaced by them.[55] The shift in Mumford's work toward locating matters of fundamental importance in American studies within the broader international discussion that marked *Technics and Civilization* is itself illustrative of the universalizing power of the machine—a key point in my own analysis. This is a primary reason for choosing this text for our own analysis. His description of the interpenetration of machine and culture continues to serve as the starting point for any comprehensive discussion of the problems of reading the Bible in an American society increasingly dominated by the machine. Here, the fundamental issues that continue to plague us were introduced to the American reading public.

---

[54]Alan Trachtenberg, "Diagnostician of the Machine Age," *Times Literary Supplement* no. 3,891 (8 October 1976) 1,301. Besides the work mentioned, this period saw the publication of the following works: *Sticks and Stones: A Study of American Architecture and Civilization* (1924), *The Golden Day: A Study in American Experience and Culture* (1926), and *Herman Melville* (1929). Trachtenberg writes, "His books of that decade . . . are classics of American studies, all the more remarkable and inspiriting for their freedom from academic narrowness, their imaginative grasp of nodal points of culture where arts and letters, politics and society, the shape of cities and regions, mutually illuminate each other and their common matrix. Mumford's range is not confined, of course, to matters American, and his works in the following decades . . . have established him as a presence on the international—certainly the Western—scene. His influence upon planning and architecture has been as notable as that upon American cultural studies. . . ."

[55]Dow makes this statement about the crucial stage in Mumford's life and work denoted by *Civilization and Technics*: "Mumford could with some justification feel in the late twenties and early thirties that he had a right henceforth to cast his projects within the European context. To understand this, we must see that the American frame of reference of his early work was, ultimately, the consequence of his birth and upbringing in a foreign country, New York City. The writers of his generation, he wrote in 1962, 'particularly those born around New York . . . were always close to Europe in thought, so close that we had to achieve our independence, like a child growing up, by finding our nearer roots in our own land' " (Mumford to Dow, 15 March 1962, quoted in Dow, "Mumford's Passage to India," 37). At least as early as 1932, Mumford had come to believe that he had achieved this. A month or so before leaving for Europe to do research for *Technics and Civilization*, he wrote the man who had been the greatest single influence on the first phase of his career, Van Wyck Brooks, that 'I know my country now and have a better right to look at Europe than I had a dozen years ago, when I first set out' " (Mumford to Brooks, March 1932. Brooks Papers, Rare Book Collection, Van Pelt Library of the University of Pennsylvania).

In describing the earliest phase of machine culture (which he terms "paleotechnic," as opposed to "neotechnic"), Mumford writes: "The fact is that in the great industrial areas of Western Europe and America and in the exploitable territories that are under the control of these centers, the paleotechnic phase is still intact and all its essential characteristics are uppermost. . . . In this persistence of paleotechnic practices the original anti-vital bias of the machine is evident: bellicose, money-centered, life-curbing, we continue to worship the twin deities, Mammon and Moloch, to say nothing of more abysmally savage tribal gods."[56] For Mumford, a savage materialism and greed had characterized American society from the start of its existence. The introduction of the machine into this society meant that these social patterns were intensified, rather than mollified. For example, the technical occupation of mining functioned as a paradigm for the remainder of mainstream American economic and social life.

> This dominant mode of exploitation became the pattern for subordinate forms of industry. The reckless, get-rich-quick, devil-take-the-hindmost attitude of the mining rushes spread everywhere: the bonanza farms of the Middle West in the United States were exploited as if they were mines, and the forests were gutted out and mined in the same fashion as the minerals that lay in their hills. And the damage to form and civilization through the prevalence of these new habits of disorderly exploitation and wasteful expenditure remained, whether or not the source of energy itself disappeared. The psychological results of carboniferous capitalism—the lowered morale, the expectation of getting something for nothing, the disregard for a balanced mode of production and consumption, the habituation to wreckage and debris as part of the normal human environment—all these results were plainly mischievous.[57]

This description of the interplay of technology, economics, and society readily illustrates Mumford's power of imaginative integration of various aspects of life. His approach to America is always within such an integrative framework.

Mumford believes that the intellectual task called for in our time is the exploration of the spiritual contributions of the machine to our culture.[58] In the specific instance of America, there was a short time in its history when one could retreat from the advancing machine.

> At the very moment life was becoming more constricted and routinized, a great safety valve for the aboriginal human impulses had been found—the raw, unexplored, and relatively uncultivated regions of America. . . . Failing to accept the destiny that the inventors and the industri-

---

[56]Mumford, *Technics and Civilization*, 264.

[57]Ibid., 158.

[58]Ibid., Introduction, 2.

alists were creating, failing to welcome the comforts and the conveniences of civilized existence and accept the high value placed upon them by the reigning bourgeoisie, those who possessed hardier virtues and a quicker sense of values could escape from the machine. . . . Here, likewise, those too weak to face the machine could find temporary refuge.[59]

Thus, the power of the machine is such that it routinizes all of life, and America had early on played the role of safety valve for those Europeans who had rebelled against this "advance" in civilization. However, in time, even America was not expansive enough to keep from its shores the mechanical sweep through civilization emanating from the Continent. The mechanical philosophy had revealed something hitherto unknown about nature, and once this revelation was made manifest, it would not again be covered.

> The specific triumph of the technical imagination rested on the ability to dissociate lifting power from the arm and create a crane: to dissociate work from the action of men and animals and create the water-mill: to dissociate light from the combustion of wood and oil and create the electric lamp. For thousands of years animism had stood in the way of this development; for it had concealed the entire face of nature behind a scrawl of human forms.[60]

The spiritual force of technology lay in its ability to penetrate nature beyond animism. Once this deeper aspect of nature was known, the old framework would never again be seen as adequate. In this sense, the very discovery and exploration of America was born and nurtured in this new technical imagination. And, in that very sense, the term America has represented a spiritual concept from its inception.

Technology in Relational Praxis. It is possible to conceive of technology in an autonomous way, as our discussion of Jacques Ellul illustrates below. The framework Mumford provides in his discussion, however, is a pluralistic approach to this subject: if technology seems monolithic, it is because of the way that it has been wedded in modern life with those elemental economic and social forces that together with it form a highly impenetrable defense against change. The real force that lies behind all these forces (technology included) is the particularly barren and sterile rationalism that has afflicted the last centuries of Western civilization. Mumford speaks of the nineteenth and twentieth centuries in the following terms: "A new type of personality had emerged, a walking abstraction: the Economic Man. Living men imitated this penny-in-the-slot automaton, this creature of bare rationalism."[61] This new rationalistic man

---

[59]Ibid., 295f.

[60]Ibid., 33.

[61]Ibid., 177.

sacrificed the older virtues of "art, play, amusement," and "pure crafts-manship" for the "gospel of work."[62] However, the new gospel promising human deliverance was a failure in the very terms and categories that it promised to deliver. Whereas it proclaimed release of the burdens of the ordinary worker, it actually increased them. As a result, there was born the necessity of ideology that would convince people of just the opposite of what was happening to them.

Mumford describes the new ideology in this way: "The central elements in that ideology were two principles that had operated like dynamite upon the solid rock of feudalism and special privilege: the principle of utility and the principle of democracy."[63] Here the three categories of technology (utility), democracy (equality), and economics (capitalism) are united under the same ideological banner. For Mumford, it would be inadequate to separate artificially one of these categories from the others. What was important was that "mass production of cheap goods merely carried the principle of democracy on the material plane. . ."[64] All three of the primary elements of technology, democracy, and capitalism are present in this one statement; and, at the center of it all was the machine, the product of abstract human reasoning. The machine had made possible mass production (technology), cheap goods (capitalism), and leveling of matter (applied democracy). This new way of viewing the world represented a configuration of human activity and thought that swept away the worldviews that preceded it. The crucial point here, however, is that Mumford understands this alliance of categories as a product of human abstraction, and not one that is inherent in them. It is for this reason that they are established as ideology, as expressions of power designed to promote the interests of the shapers of civilization. He therefore concludes, "Although capitalism and technics must be clearly distinguished at every stage, one conditioned the other and reacted upon it."[65] Thus, it would be a mistake to view the actual development of the machine in American civilization as intrinsic to the machine itself. Rather,

it was . . . unfortunate that the machine was conditioned, at the outset, by these foreign institutions [of trade] and took on characteristics that had nothing essentially to do with the technical processes or the forms of work. Capitalism utilized the machine, not to further social welfare, but to increase private profit: mechanical instruments were used for the aggrandizement of the ruling classes. . . . Enough here to notice the close historical association of modern technics and modern capitalism, and to point out

---

[62]Ibid., 176.

[63]Ibid., 177.

[64]Ibid., 178.

[65]Ibid., 26.

that, for all this historical development, *there is no necessary connection between them* [my emphasis].[66]

Because the connection between technical development and economics was an external and artificial one, it is necessary in the analysis of technics to separate it from this secondary relationship. Mumford continues, "It was because of certain traits in private capitalism that the machine—which was a neutral agent—has often seemed, and in fact has sometimes been, a malicious element in society, careless of human life, indifferent to human interests. The machine has suffered for the sins of capitalism; contrariwise, capitalism has often taken credit for the virtues of the machine."[67] Technics, Mumford thereby maintains, must be interpreted in terms of the economic structure that prepares the ground for it, and that nurtures its development in certain well-defined ways. This primacy of economics over technics, however, is one that is established historically, not essentially or metaphysically.

Mumford does not maintain that the technological imagination is generated by economics (or democracy) alone. The ground for this worldview had to be established in a particular mentality, or way of being. He therefore observes most succinctly, "The mechanization of human habits prepared the way for mechanical imitations."[68] By this he means that something existed in Western history prior to the ascendancy of the technical way of life: man himself, it seems, had become mechanical before he had perfected his machines. While Mumford sees the roots of this process in the mechanization of *time*, (a point I will develop below), it was during the time of the the Middle Ages that the process began in earnest. The theology of the Middle Ages had disparaged the body, a perception of world and humanity that carried the unforeseen result of the intellectual construction of a major pathway of the machine into human consciousness. Mumford notes,

> Hating the body, the orthodox minds of the Middle Ages were prepared to do it violence. *Instead of resenting the machines that could counterfeit this or that action of the body, they could welcome them.* The forms of the machine were no more ugly or repulsive than the bodies of crippled and battered men and women, or, if they were repulsive and ugly, they were that much further away from being a temptation to the flesh. . . . [Therefore] *in spite of itself, the Church was creating devil's disciples* [my emphasis].[69]

It was this suspicion and distaste for the flesh, therefore, that philosoph-

---

[66]Ibid., 26–27.

[67]Ibid., 27.

[68]Ibid., 41.

[69]Ibid., 36.

ically (and theologically) prepared the ground for a greatly accelerated mechanical habit of mind that led to the advanced machine age of our own time. As the Middle Ages advanced, and the body was increasingly disparaged, men became more attracted to "the methodical routine of the drillmaster and the book-keeper, the soldier and the bureaucrat."[70] By the time of the seventeenth century, these "masters of regimentation" had gained full cultural ascendency. I might add that the era of the birth and definition of the American republic is to be viewed in the context of this general Western social development. Whatever else America had the potential to become, its destiny lay in living out the script of those intellectual parameters that came to the forefront of European society—a destiny that earmarked it as the harbinger of the new technology.

Mumford believes that from the religious side, one particular fact accompanied the rise of the mechanical philosophy, namely, the loss of traditional faith. But before that, Protestantism had already begun the process of baptizing Christianity into the new way of thinking. "The peculiar office of Protestantism was to unite finance to the concept of a godly life and to turn the asceticism countenanced by religion into a device for concentration upon worldly goods and worldly advancement. *Protestantism rested firmly on the abstractions of print and money*" [my emphasis].[71] Mumford describes Protestantism as developing in a world in which the medieval synthesis was in the process of crumbling. Its success was due primarily to the degree that it adapted from the new, its power and validity in what the new contributed to the recent symbiosis of faith and culture. This description of the times is representative.

> Men no longer believed, without practical reservations, in heaven and hell and the communion of the saints. . . . Observe the infant Jesus of a thirteenth century altarpiece: the infant lies on an altar, apart; the Virgin is transfixed and beatified by the presence of the Holy Ghost: the myth is real. Observe the Holy Families of the sixteenth and seventeenth century painting: fashionable young ladies are coddling their well-fed human infants: the myth has died. First only the gorgeous clothes are left: finally a doll takes the place of the living child: a mechanical puppet. *Mechanics became the new religion, and it gave the world a new Messiah: the machine* [author's emphasis].[72]

Perhaps no statement more deeply touches the heart of Mumford's argument and is of greater relevance to the concerns of the present book than this last sentence. This insight into the intellectual forces comprising the present time is central to the problem of biblical hermeneutics in the Amer-

---

[70]Ibid., 42.

[71]Ibid., 43.

[72]Ibid., 45.

ican setting and the mechanical messianism that has accompanied its development. As indicated above, Mumford argues that we are still living according to the precepts of the "paleotechnic age" when the machine is dominated by "anti-vital" characteristics. The rapid ascendancy of the mechanical worldview was greatly accelerated in the West by the spiritual vacuum left by the dissipation of religious faith. In times of intellectual chaos, such as that engendered by the loss of the medieval synthesis, humans are attracted by absolutes. The new philosophy was strong precisely where the culture was weak, and a new generation of priests of regimentation had arisen to inculcate the new religion. Indeed, the old faith could survive in vital form only if it sold its soul to mechanical messianism.

The context in which modern technology developed upon its inception in the West is determinative for its character, and it must, therefore, be viewed in relational terms. Mumford consistently maintains that while the machine is ethically a neutral category, he noted in the 1963 introduction to *Technics and Civilization* that there exist "regressive possibilities of many of our most hopeful technical advances." As a result, he congratulates himself on foreseeing from early on "the ominous linkage, as I put it later, between the 'Automaton' and the 'Id.' "[73] By its very nature, the technical imagination is *associational*; it invites adaption and utilization by another. Capitalism, which Mumford understands as promoting the interests of the id, has historically used the technical imagination to promote its own interests. It has redefined technology from being an instrument of life, to becoming an absolute in its own terms.[74] Yet in spite of all the particular ways that things have developed in the West, "there is no necessary connection between them."[75] Technology is in its essence ambiguous. Mumford concludes, "One is confronted, then, by the fact that the machine is ambivalent. It is both an instrument of liberation and one of repression. It has economized human energy and it has misdirected it. It has created a wide framework of order and it has produced muddle and chaos. It has nobly served human purposes and it has distorted and denied them."[76] The challenge is to construct a new philosophy (and theology) that will adequately adjust to the newly found power of the machine, and not be weak at the very point where the latter is strong. The failure to do so portends the gravest consequences for the human condition. "The failure of 'adjustment' may be looked upon as a failure of art and morals and religion to change with the same degree of rapidity as the machine and to change in the same direction, when it hap-

---

[73] Ibid., Introduction, 5.

[74] Ibid., 281.

[75] Ibid., 27.

[76] Ibid., 283.

pens the machine is taking a course that would, unless compensated, lead to human deterioration and collapse."[77] I know of no more compelling reason to address the problem of self-consciously reading the Bible in the context of American civilization in order to establish a truly vital dialogue between it and ourselves. The task remains to locate the ground of the technological imagination, so that we can better determine the means by which we can relate it to the root document of our religious heritage. In this regard, Mumford points us in the direction of the central significance of the mechanical view of time with penetrating insight.

The Mechanics of Time. In a statement that carries the greatest significance for his analysis of the technical imagination, Mumford writes, "The clock, not the steam-engine, is the key-machine of the modern industrial age."[78] As might be expected from this statement, his description of the inter-relationship between time and technology is at the heart of his philosophy of technology. In tracing the origins of the impact of mechanical time on technological development, Mumford locates Western monasteries as a central contributing factor due to the emphasis on order and power found there "after the long uncertainty and bloody confusion that attended the breakdown of the Roman Empire."[79] Not only did the monks make a major contribution to the emerging mechanical philosophy by "the iron discipline of the rule" and the daily regulated canonical hours, but Mumford entertains the idea that the Benedictines were the founders of modern capitalism itself. At any rate, "their rule certainly took the curse off work and their vigorous engineering enterprises may even have robbed warfare of some of its glamor."[80] He summarizes as follows: "So one is not straining the facts when one suggests that the monasteries—at one time there were 40,000 under the Benedictine rule—helped to give human enterprise the regular collective beat and rhythm of the machine; for *the clock is not merely a means of keeping track of the hours, but of synchronizing the actions of men*" [my emphasis].[81]

Once again we find the overriding interest of Mumford to trace modern technics back to a frame of mind, or a way of thinking. He correctly holds that the way we approach time (and space) is determined culturally. Thus, behind the clock stands a way of thinking. To evaluate the clock and its effects on the way we look at life, one must penetrate to that particular way of thinking. The key point here is "no two cultures live conceptually in the same kind of time and space. Space and time, like lan-

---

[77] Ibid., 316–17.

[78] Ibid., 14.

[79] In general, see ibid., 12–18 for a discussion of "The Monastery and the Clock."

[80] Ibid., 13.

[81] Ibid., 13-14.

guage itself, are works of art, and like language they help condition and direct practical action."[82] As Immanuel Kant had correctly maintained, time and space were not "out there" as such, but were categories of the human mind. The clock is, we might say, a mechanical hermeneutics of time. It must be evaluated as such.

What is the philosophical significance of the emergence of mechanical time in Western consciousness? It lies in this fact: "By its essential nature it dissociated time from human events and helped create the belief in an independent world of mathematically measurable sequences: the special world of science."[83] Mechanical time, with its emphasis on cyclical regularity, carried with it the new possibility of interpreting time abstractly, without recourse to human reality. It is, in short, the intellectualization of time. Mumford contrasts this view with "organic time." A major difference between the two views exists in the question of the reversibility or irreversibility of time: "Though mechanical time can, in a sense, be speeded up or run backward, like the hands of a clock or the images of a moving picture, organic time moves in only one direction—through the cycle of birth, growth, development, decay, and death—and the past that is already dead remains present in the future that has still to be born."[84]

The reality to which this insightful statement points, but is not fully developed by Mumford, is that mechanical time opens the possibility of the rational dissection and manipulation of time. When one replaces the conception of time as being tied to the living body, with one grounded in the regulated movement of a machine, time is intellectualized and is removed a step further away from the natural world. Now one takes "the past," "the present," and "the future" as realities that exist in nature, thus obscuring that they are rational constructs that do not exist there at all, but merely in the human mind. As Mumford comments, "Now, the orderly punctual life that first took shape in the monasteries is not native to mankind, although by now Western peoples are so thoroughly regimented by the clock that it is 'second nature' and they look upon its observance as a fact of nature." This taking of "second nature" as "nature" itself, is the fundamental flaw that was introduced into Western consciousness during the rise of the mechanical philosophy, and it still represents a problem that stands at the heart of the American experience. The crucial point to be remembered is: "mechanical time is not an absolute."[85] It serves a utilitarian function; but it is not absolute. Further drawing out the implications of the artificiality of mechanical time toward the end of

---

[82]Ibid., 18.

[83]Ibid., 15.

[84]Ibid., 16.

[85]Ibid., 271.

the book, Mumford makes this salient point: "The technique of creating a neutral world of fact as distinguished from the raw data of immediate experience was the great general contribution of modern analytic science. . . . The concept of a neutral world, untouched by man's efforts, indifferent to his activities, obdurate to his wish and supplication, is one of the great triumphs of man's imagination, and in itself it represents a fresh human value." The abstraction of time carried with it the seeds of the neutralization of nature. But, just as animism had itself been an interpretation of nature, a reading into the raw data of nature by the human intellect, so too, was the new mechanical philosophy. The new conception of a regularized, impersonal nature was just as imaginative as the older, spiritualized nature. Perhaps it was more imaginative, in the sense that the operation of the rational mind was more evident than ever before. But, in either case, man was increasingly able to conceptualize himself more and more apart from natural processes, and this fact by itself changed the way he looked at everything, including his religion.

One of the important philosophical and theological consequences of the medieval conception of space and time was the belief in the religious order as the connecting link between events: " . . . the true order of space was Heaven, even as the true order of time was Eternity."[86] This divine order broke down with the rise of mechanical time. The result was that "both Eden and Heaven were outside the new space. . . ." This loss of the religious perspective in the interpretation of the world carried the greatest of ramifications for the emerging technical worldview. "The categories of time and space, once practically dissociated, had become united: and the abstractions of measured time and measured space undermined the earlier conceptions of infinity and eternity. . . . The itch to *use* [author's emphasis] space and time had broken out: and once they were coordinated with movement, they could be contracted or expanded: the conquest of space and time had begun" [author's emphasis].[87] At its core, then, the mechanization of time (and space) carries the onus of the reduction of the raw data of the universe to *pure utility*, which is at the center of the technological imagination. This, in turn, had the greatest of ramifications for general cultural values. "Value, in the doctrine of progress, was reduced to a time-calculation: value was in fact *movement in time*. To be old-fashioned or to be 'out of date' was to lack value" [author's emphasis].[88] Once time and space had become quantified according to the dictates of progress in this way, the path was open for their redefinition in terms of both the commercialization (capitalism)[89] and measurement

---

[86]Ibid., 19–20.

[87]Ibid., 22.

[88]Ibid., 183–84.

[89]Ibid., 197.

for utilitarian means and ends (technology) of these categories. These are the approaches that dominate in the last several hundred years in the area of Western hermeneutics of nature, the apogee of which has characterized the American experience.

The results of the mechanical reinterpretation of time and space carried the direst consequences for the way life would be conceived and carried out in the West. Mumford continues, "What was left was the bare, depopulated world of matter and motion: a wasteland. . . . Indeed in this empty, denuded world, the invention of machines became a duty. By renouncing a large part of his humanity, a man could achieve godhood: he dawned on this second chaos and created the machine in his own image: the image of power, but power ripped loose from his flesh and isolated from his humanity."[90] The imaginative penetration of the mechanical mind into space and time that had begun in the Middle Ages further intensified the process of man's *disincarnation* of his own humanity for which the disparagement of the flesh in the Middle Ages discussed above had prepared the ground. The result was an awesome mixture of intellectual, spiritual, and emotional beliefs that propelled the machine to the center of the world stage. If the machine were not divine, it was surely divinelike. The specific point of contact between man and God that the machine provided was that of *power*: all of the religious aspirations that had traditionally informed Western civilization had become focused in this one overriding reality. The machine takes on theological significance in our lives once we locate its development in this particular cultural context. Power itself is nothing less than an abstraction and, as such, is antithetical to the major thrust of Christian thought. The correct theological countermovement to power is the reestablishment of the primacy of the body: whether this be the power of the machine, or the even more abstracted form of power that the machine engenders in societal relationships. This carries with it the de-abstraction of time, and the restoration of some sense of the unity and fullness of "organic" time.

For Mumford, therefore, the machine as such is not an unmitigated evil in the world, in spite of the dangerous precipice to which it has brought us. It has the potential of being modified and restored to its proper role in society, if, and only if, traditional Western values can be restored to their rightful place. But this cannot be done simply by restating the old truths. The new mechanical way of conceiving time carried the means by which it might be filled and emptied at will. If time could be speeded up instrumentally by human reason, then the demands on the old traditions would be severely strained. It is only by momentous effort that this challenge might be met. The ambiguity of the situation lay in this fact: should the mechanical challenge be successfully met by the tradition, then not

---

[90]Ibid., 51.

only might we stave off our own destruction, but the tradition itself would be immeasurably enriched. The question remains to be discussed in what precisely lay the positive features of the technical imagination onto which the Western tradition might be attached? It is to a consideration of this matter that I now turn.

The Spirituality of Technology. Granted that mechanical time is not an absolute reality, and that industrialized technology is fraught with the problems of inhuman practices, it can be argued with much justification that the most desirable course of action is the return to a pretechnical age. Are not the problems simply too great to be mastered? Indeed, Mumford's litany of problematical features of our modern machine civilization is imposing: "The regularization of time, the increase in mechanical power, the multiplication of goods, the contraction of time and space, the standardization of performance and product, the transfer of skill to automata, and the increase of collective interdependence. . . ."[91] The commonalty of all of these characteristics is a certain alienation from the primary experiences of life. Whatever time is, it is more than the regular beat of mechanical clockwork. The mechanical multiplication of goods is similarly unnatural, as are the standardized measurements of performance and product. The way in which the running of the machine causes the worker to relinquish his or her skill to the point at which this skill actually becomes a negative factor that impedes the productive process is a further dissociation of mechanics with primary human experience. If the technical process is a veil that stands between humans and the fullness of life for which they are naturally destined, is it not in the best interest of all that the veil be removed?

With regard to this crucial question, Mumford was of the absolute conviction that there was no possibility of turning back the technological clock, nor would such a result be ultimately desirable. The reasoning that he provides directs us to a view of the technical imagination that we may regard as spiritual in implication. In developing his views, after devoting a large portion of his book to the development of the machine in the West, he recounts in a rather lengthy chapter those societal elements that have historically run counter to the machine and have opposed it. All of these antitechnological tendencies, however, have failed in their efforts to restore earlier models of human existence. The most obvious attempts to reject the influx of the machine in daily life are to be associated generally with the concept of *romanticism*. While acknowledging the complexities of the romantic reaction to the machine, Mumford limits his own detailed considerations to "the three dominant forms: the cult of history and nationalism, the cult of nature, and the cult of the primitive." Other movements grounded in romanticism are "the cult of the isolated individual,

---

[91]Ibid., 281.

and the revival of old theologies and theosophies and supernatural-isms." He remarks that since it is "next to impossible to distinguish clearly between the continued interests of religion and their modern revivals," he will confine himself to "romanticism proper."[92] Clearly, the important point that he makes throughout this section is that all these efforts fail in their goal of halting the spread of technology; indeed, they are all doomed to failure. This is as true of romanticized religion as it is of the more sec-ularized varieties. It remains to answer the question of why this is, or *must be*, the case.

The specific reason romanticism must fail is that the machine call forth genuine human values and takes on the character of a pedagogue in dis-persing these values to society. In fact, the machine has functioned as a "constant instrument of discipline and education" from generation to generation. Mumford notes, "If the machine had really lacked cultural values, the Romantics would have been right, and their desire to seek these values, if need be, in a dead past would have been justified by the very desperateness of the case."[93] It was, therefore, the intrinsically valid contributions of the machine to culture that ultimately thwarted any at-tempt to turn it back from the sweep of human history. Mumford goes so far as to propose that technics may be producing "a third estate between nature and the humane arts."[94] What are the contributions to culture that more explicitly might make up this "third estate"? What specific lessons has the machine taught? The obvious ones are increased emphasis on the factual and the practical. These are the characteristics of the machine that the "industrialist made the sole key to intelligence." But beyond these as-pects, Mumford calls our attention to

> the technique of cooperative thought and action it has fostered, the es-thetic excellence of the machine forms, the delicate logic of materials and forces, which has added a new canon—the machine canon—to the arts: above all, perhaps, the more objective personality that has come into ex-istence through a more sensitive and understanding intercourse with these new social instruments and through their deliberate cultural assimilation. *In projecting one side of the human personality into the concrete forms of the ma-chine, we have created an independent environment that has reacted upon every other side of the personality* [author's emphasis].[95]

Of the several positive aspects of the machine that this statement sug-gests, the one Mumford himself most convincingly develops is mechan-ical esthetics. In a subsequent discussion, for example, he recognizes the

---

[92]Ibid., 287.

[93]Ibid., 323.

[94]Ibid., 322.

[95]Ibid., 324.

"relatively new esthetic terms: precision, calculation, flawlessness, simplicity, economy. . . . " Of these categories, he considers the principle of economy to be the chief esthetic principle. Success with the machine means the elimination of the nonessential, whereas in handicraft, it is the "willing production of superfluity, contributed by the worker out of his own delight in the work." The result is that "in handicraft it is the worker who is represented: in machine design it is the work."[96]

Mumford only imperfectly develops the positive aspects of technology given above at the conclusion of his book. They are subsidiary to his main purpose and effectively remain for the reader to ponder and consider more completely. As my discussion has indicated, it is not the primary intention of Mumford to explore in a definitive way the positive contributions of technology to civilization. His purpose is much more to argue for the liberation of the modern technical imagination from its capitalistic and military roots, and point toward its integration into the tradition of Western values. In order for this to happen, it is necessary to establish the inherent worth of the machine in its own right. The failure of Western philosophy—taken in its broadest sense—to face up to the positive aspects of the machine, and to hide behind a thinly thought-out, antitechnological posture, is really a reflection of its own inability or unwillingness to grow and mature. A statement like the one made above that propels the machine into philosophy and the humanities is central to the structure of Mumford's argument because he intends to liberate both them *and* the technical imagination. In this way, it is his intention to free us from the old mechanistic worldview that propelled the machine into contemporary society with such force, *but not from machines as such*.

There does, therefore, exist a legitimate place for machines in our lives. The exact place is described in these terms: "The chief benefit the rational use of the machine promises is certainly not the elimination of work: what it promises is something quite different—the elimination of *servile* work or *slavery*: those types of work that deform the body, cramp the mind, deaden the spirit" [author's emphasis].[97] The human condition is such that work like this will always be present. Hence, the necessity of machines, and the promise of human liberation that they hold. But, in order for the machine to fulfill this destiny, it must itself be liberated from its capitalistic and old mechanical (paleotechnic) cultural context. Mumford observes, "Thanks to capitalism, the machine has been over-worked, over-enlarged, over-exploited because of the possibility of making money out of it."[98] And, again, "The emphasis in the future must be, not upon speed

---

[96]Ibid., 350.

[97]Ibid., 414.

[98]Ibid., 367.

and immediate practical conquest, but upon exhaustiveness, inter-relationship, and integration."[99] Once, in other words, the technical imagination is left free to be simply that—technical imagination—then the true values to civilization that lie embedded ambiguously within it will come to the fore. The result, surprising as this may sound in our present society, will be that the machine will fulfill its own interior logic and become "to a great degree self-eliminating."[100] In this way, Mumford wishes to point us to the cutting edge of the human adventure with the machine, its interrelationship with life itself. In that sense, the perfection of the machine implies in large measure its own disappearance.

Orwell / On Power as Political Apotheosis

The pencil felt thick and awkward in his fingers. He began to write down the thoughts that came into his head. He wrote first in large clumsy capitals:
                    FREEDOM IS SLAVERY.
Then almost without a pause he wrote beneath it:
                    TWO AND TWO MAKE FIVE.
But then there came a sort of check. His mind, as though shying away from something, seemed unable to concentrate. He knew that he knew what came next, but for the moment he could not recall it. When he did recall it, it was only by consciously reasoning out what it must be; it did not come of its own accord. He wrote:
                    GOD IS POWER.[101]

Introduction.* While Mumford's discussion of "technics" is classic for addressing the place of the machine in the New World garden, the study is only suggestive in drawing out the full philosophical implications of the relation of the machine to other spheres of human activity. For example, we see that the failure of democracy to liberate the machine from the corrupting force of capitalism becomes apocalyptic vision in George Orwell's political novel *1984*. Democracy had liberated the machine, and now the machine has loosed pure, raw power that has taken up residence in the political body. In the society Orwell depicts, the Party not only controls the machine, but it becomes the machine in an unprecedented display of efficient power. In order to maintain this power, it is essential that the Party controls the machinery of its society. Thus, for Orwell, writing little more than a century later than Tocqueville, democracy as such was also no absolute guarantee against political tyranny.

---

[99]Ibid., 372.

[100]Ibid., 428.

[101]George Orwell, *1984* (New York: New American Library, 1984) 228.

*Pages 58–81 appeared in abbreviated form in an article entitled "The Fragility of Time: Orwell and Ellul in the Matrix of Theological Origins," in Frederick Ferré, ed., *Technology and Religion*, vol. 10 of *Research in Philosophy and Technology* (Greenwich CT, London: JAI Press, 1990) 129–48. Reprinted by permission from JAI Press.

In the midst of the popularity of *1984* among American readers, it is not commonly known that one of the major totalitarian powers in Orwell's popular novel is the United States—Tocqueville's cradle of democracy. In the novel, Orwell explains the development of world totalitarianism in this way:

> The splitting-up of the world into three great super-states was an event which could be and indeed was foreseen before the middle of the twentieth century. With the absorption of Europe by Russia *and the British Empire by the United States,* two of the three existing powers, Eurasia and Oceania, were already effectively in being. . . . Oceania comprises the Americas, the Atlantic islands including the British Isles, Australasia, and the southern portion of Africa" [my emphasis]. [102]

Britain carries the name Airstrip One and functions as an American outpost on the edge of the Continent, an area controlled by Russia. These two superpowers—Oceania and Eurasia—exist in a state of perpetual warfare, along with the third great power Eastasia (China and the countries to the south). Importantly, the great powers of *1984* are no longer "divided by any genuine ideological difference." Thus, for Orwell, it is false to juxtapose democracy and totalitarianism. He had the advantage of viewing democracy matured by more than a century than did Tocqueville. Yet, his vision is, in a real sense, the natural unfolding of Tocqueville's growing fear of democracy. Whereas the latter could only imagine the apathy and loss of liberty that centralization would bring, the former presupposed that and directed his intention, instead, to the offspring of an unfettered democracy—the infamous Party. The Party represents, so to speak, the extraction of pure democratic rationality that has become pure mythos: the democratic impulses of individualism and centralization of which Tocqueville warned, bereft of all mitigating social contact and conscience. It was the embodiment of the fears of both Tocqueville and Mumford in its most unadulterated form within the political realm.

Orwell's intentions in writing *1984* are clearly manifest by his own descriptive statement.

> My recent novel is NOT intended as an attack on socialism or on the British Labour Party (of which I am a supporter) but as a show-up of the perversions to which a centralized economy is liable and which have already been realized in Communism and Fascism. I do not believe that the kind of society I describe *necessarily* will arrive, but I believe (allowing of course for the fact that the book is a satire) that something resembling it *could* arrive. [103]

---

[102]Ibid., 153.

[103]Quoted in Irving Howe, "*1984:* Enigmas of Power," in Howe, ed., *1984 Revisited: Totalitarianism in Our Century* (New York: Harper & Row, 1983) 18.

By way of background, a few years before the appearance of *1984* Orwell had observed that "every line of serious work that I have written since 1936 has been written, directly or indirectly, *against* totalitarianism and *for* democratic socialism, as I understand it."[104] In his own experience, the Spanish Civil War was the watershed event that "politicized" art and knowledge. Therefore, it is indisputable that *1984* is first and foremost a political novel, more specifically, a novel of political power and corruption. Lionel Trilling's description is quite apt: "The exposition of the *mystique* of power is the heart and essence of Orwell's book."[105] As O'Brien, speaking as a Party spokesman, informs Winston Smith in the book, "Power is not a means; it is an end."[106] Therefore, while the fabric of the storyline is woven with the materials of the modern or postmodern industrial state, no definitive answer is given to the vexing question of whether or not industrialization itself necessarily leads to the political corruptions it depicts.[107] Rather, Orwell's book is not a prophecy, it is a warning. He describes for us what *might* become the ultimate development of the democratic state *if* we sufficiently lower our vigilance vis-à-vis the efficiency advancing technology affords the corrupt who can assume power. It is, we might say, the story of the marriage of democracy and technology, and the inability of the former to control the efficient power of the latter.

The Politicization of Technique. In spite of the fact that *1984* is not a novel about technology per se, it does provide us with some provocative thoughts on this subject within the political sphere. As I have indicated, the book must be placed in the context of Orwell's overriding political interest. First of all, it is clear that he was acutely aware of the revolution the machine brought to societal structures. The machine represented a danger to the status quo of class society. A quote from the book written by Emmanuel Goldstein held as heretical by the Party in *1984* (entitled *The Theory and Practice of Oligarchical Collectivism*) illustrates this point.

> From the moment when the machine first made its appearance it was

---

[104]George Orwell, "Why I Write," in *A Collection of Essays* (New York: Harcourt Brace Jovanovich, 1946) 314.

[105]Lionel Trilling, "Orwell on the Future," in C. J. Kuppig, ed., *Nineteen Eighty-Four to 1984* (New York: Carroll & Graf, 1984) 162.

[106]Orwell, *1984*, 175.

[107]Richard Rees believes that Orwell does answer this question. He writes, "The core of Orwell's message in *1984*, stripped of Winston's tragedy and all the sadism, is simply that our industrial machine civilization is tending to deracinate and debilitate us, and will finally destroy us." Cf. Rees, "All or Nothing," in Kuppig, *Nineteen Eighty-Four*, 222. I find this statement overly simplistic in that it does not address the underlying forces at play in modern industrial technology.

clear to all thinking people that the need for human drudgery, and therefore to a great extent for human inequality, had disappeared. If the machine were used deliberately for that end, hunger, overwork, dirt, illiteracy,
and disease could be eliminated within a few generations. . . . But it was
also clear that an all-round increase in wealth threatened the destruction—
indeed, in some sense was the destruction—of a hierarchical society.[108]

If a solution is to be found for the present human predicament, it lies in
the liberation of the machine for the release from human drudgery and
inequality. *1984* describes how the threatened power class, embodied in
the Party, successfully maintains its control over the natural development of the machine. Now, Mumford's vision of the failure of philosophy and humanistic study to mollify and inform the extraordinary power
of the machine here becomes an imaginative reality. The Party utilizes
techniques of oppression that are ultimately derived from the machine to
ward off the powerless in the social realm that is spawned by the machine
in the technical realm. Orwell continues (in the voice of Goldstein),

> In the long run, a hierarchical society was only possible on a basis of
> poverty and ignorance. To return to the agricultural past, as some thinkers
> about the beginning of the twentieth century dreamed of doing, was not a
> practicable solution. It conflicted with the tendency toward mechanization
> which had become quasi-instinctive throughout almost the whole world,
> and moreover, any country which remained industrially backward was
> helpless in a military sense and was bound to be dominated, directly or
> indirectly, by its more advanced rivals.[109]

In the spirit of Mumford, Orwell does not seek a solution to the problems
of the modern industrial world by retreating to naturalism or romanticism. This is because the machine itself, by the mid-twentieth century,
had become a "quasi-instinctive" part of human nature. It could no longer
be arbitrarily removed. Orwell recognized this as the given quality of human existence in our time from which even art itself must proceed.

However, the promise for good that had accompanied and nurtured
the modern machine from its inception had failed to materialize in the
twentieth century. Two world wars had painfully born out this fact. In
commenting on *1984*, Alfred Kazin puts the matter succinctly.

> Just at the moment when twentieth-century technology had shown it-
> self capable of feeding the hungry when unencumbered, everything in sight
> justified Marx's testimony in The Communist Manifesto to the power of
> new productive forces and Whitehead's praise of "the century of hope" for
> "inventing invention," socialism in its original meaning—the end of tribal
> nationalism, of man's alienation from his own essence, of wealth deter-

---

[108]Orwell, *1984*, 126.

[109]Ibid., 126–27.

mining all values in society—yielded to the nightmare of coercion.[110]

What had gone wrong with the technological dream? Why had technology "yielded to the nightmare of coercion"? For Orwell, the answer seems to lie in the fact that technology had lost its way because it had severed those primal intellectual associations that had initially fostered its development. Such associations were deemed *oldspeak* by the Party, concepts such as *free*[dom], *honor, justice, morality, internationalism, democracy, science,* and *religion.* In Orwell's terms, these words were all grouped "round the concepts of objectivity and rationalism."[111] By implication, therefore, technology embedded in the context of objectivity and rationality offered the single greatest hope of mankind. Perhaps the term *science* comes closest to capturing the essence of this view, if we conceive of the term in the broad sense of the free pursuit of knowledge according to rational and objective means. But totalitarianism had co-opted rational science and displaced its primary relationship with technology. As David Goodman writes, "The governments of *1984* are able to exercise such strict control over their citizens largely because they have adapted the fruits of science and technology to their own ends."[112] Similarly, George Woodcock notes that in the novel "science is *diverted* to producing refined instruments of torture, industry feeds a perpetual war that engenders the hatred on which power rests" [my emphasis].[113] Whether one speaks of "adapting" or "diverting," the end result is much the same. Technology has failed in *1984* because it has not been allowed to run its full, unencumbered course. Technology had become, in effect, antitechnology through the corrupting power of the Party.

Time as Palimpsest. Faced with the liberating threat of technology, the Party's strategy was, in effect, to redirect the threat back upon itself.[114] The natural development of technology is arrested by the Party by turning politically controlled technology against it. In order to accomplish this, two aspects of human rationality are singled out by Orwell as fundamental to totalitarian control: language and time. By controlling language, the

---

[110]Alfred Kazin, "Not One of Us," *New York Review of Books* 31:10 (14 June 1984): 14.

[111]Orwell, *1984,* 201.

[112]David Goodman, "Countdown to 1984: Big Brother May Be Right on Schedule," in Kuppig, *Nineteen Eighty-Four,* 294.

[113]George Woodcock, "Utopias in Negative," ibid., 87.

[114]Kenneth J. Arrow points out that the Party does not even use all the technology available to it. This is seen, for example, in the fact that Orwell portrays an economy that has retrogressed from its prewar levels. Arrow, "The Economics of *Nineteen Eighty-Four,*" in Peter Stansky, ed., *On "Nineteen Eighty-Four"* (New York: W. H. Freeman, 1983) 44.

Party put itself in the position of controlling the human perception of time. By manipulating these two cognitive spheres, the politicization of technology was complete, and absolute power lay securely in the hands of the Party. At this point, Orwell is in basic agreement with Josiah Royce, who argues that the temporal order is the exteriorization of the life of the interpretive will. He writes, "What we mean by future time is a realm of events which we view as more or less under the control of the present will of voluntary agents."[115] The Party had recognized that its political grip on the people depended on its abiltity to control their interpretation of past, present, and future.

Hermeneutical control of the temporal order makes possible a new way of thinking that alienates technological advancement from its native rational context and sets it in a new mythological one. Orwell terms the new irrational context *doublethink*, a twilight world in which one holds "two contradictory beliefs in one's mind simultaneously," and accepts both of them as true.[116] Doublethink is the means by which the Party absolutely politicizes all aspects of human experience, including technology and religion. Specifically, language in the hands of the Party becomes transformed into the tyrannical technology of "communications and management."[117] Through the epistemological control of human thought processes that language naturally affords it, the Party extracts the rationality from technology in surgical fashion. Presupposed at this point is the insight that language/rationality operates fundamentally by means of *differentiation*. Rationality allows us to distinguish one thing from another by establishing separate, individual identities. It is precisely this power of differentiation that totalitarianism fears in its drive toward uniformity. Commenting on Winston Smith's reiterated phrase "it made no difference" found throughout the novel, Mark Crispin Miller writes,

> This is what the Party wants to do, what it has all but accomplished—to *make no difference*, to eternalize its own rigid hierarchy by wiping out all dissidence, eccentricity, variety, comparison. . . . The Party plans to make no difference whatsoever; and each time Winston Smith employs the phrase, each time he thus reveals that he cannot conceive some difference, he thereby wins a little victory for the Party, fulfilling, in his fatalism, the Party's program of complete erasure.[118]

This is the reason that language is one of the last issues to be contended between social democracy and totalitarianism: language determines

---

[115]Josiah Royce, *The Problem of Christianity* (Chicago and London: University of Chicago Press, 1968) 288.

[116]Orwell, *1984*, 176.

[117]Lawrence Malkin, "Halfway to 1984," in Kuppig, *Nineteen Eighty-Four*, 121.

[118]Mark Crispin Miller, "The Fate of *1984*," in Howe, *"1984" Revisited*, 28.

whether or not we have a way to visualize differentiation. In this sense, all of the issues that we have been discussing—democracy, machines, and technique—in Orwell's view become increasingly reduced to a question of language in the present time. This explains his intensified interest in the subject in *1984*, embodied in the book's appendix entitled "The Principles of Newspeak."

Orwell's work encourages us to make clear distinctions within the individual categories of democracy, mechanics, technique, and even religion itself, in order to approach them from an enlightened standpoint in today's world. He reminds us that these rational, symbolic constructions are not absolutes in and of themselves. How we conceive of them and our relationship to them is the ultimate question. In the appendix Orwell notes, "Newspeak was designated not to extend but to *diminish* the range of thought, and this purpose was indirectly assisted by cutting the choice of words down to a minimum."[119] In this regard, for example, Ellul's description of technique analyzed below may already betray the narrow way that technology is perceived today. Ironically, it may already represent a sort of victory for Newspeak. The question is, does the particular form of technology that dominates in the late twentieth century carry the implication that we have exhausted the depth of meaning of technology as such? If we find certain aspects of that technology oppressive, does that carry the implication that technology as such is oppressive? Orwell denies this way of forcing the issue in an either/or way of thinking. To fail to differentiate is to fall victim to those very same forces one wishes to oppose. Only a thoroughly technologized mentality gives the choice "technology or no technology." If Orwell is correct, and we fail to differentiate a technology embedded in the power of the state from the natural human impulse to create, the more nearly we ourselves already embody a totalitarian mentality. In this case, the battle for human freedom is already lost at the conceptual level prior to the formation of societal norms.

Through the power of doublethink, the Party laid hold of the central tenet of its rationality: "the mutability of the past."[120] The Orwellian insight is that time is not simply external to human existence, but it is mediated to us by means of language. In this mediation, or hermeneutics of time, the Party had virtually eliminated time as an autonomous reality outside its own subjective interpretation: " 'Who controls the past,' ran the Party slogan, 'controls the future: who controls the present controls the past.' "[121] The sphere of time is viewed as an interrelated unity, with the entry point for Party interpretation being the control of the present.

---

[119]Orwell, *1984*, 198.

[120]Ibid., 176.

[121]Ibid., 32.

Those who controlled the present could rewrite the past, and this rewriting of the past programmed the future. The Party saw that "all history was a palimpsest, scraped clean and reinscribed exactly as often as was necessary."[122] The key to political control, therefore, was essentially linguistic, and ultimately metaphysical,—namely, the present stranglehold the Party maintained by the function of historical record keeping. By maintaining its grip on the past through the manipulation of the public perception of it, the Party remained inviolable.

> Past events, it is argued, have no objective existence, but survive only in written records and in human memories. The past is whatever the records and the memories agree upon. And since the Party is in full control of all records, and in equally full control of the minds of its members, it follows that the past is whatever the Party chooses to make it. . . . When it has been recreated in whatever shape is needed at the moment, then this new version *is* the past, and no different past can ever have existed.[123]

The real terror of the Orwellian vision now comes to light. It does not stop at simple totalitarian control of human behavior. If so, it would be a matter for political science and theory. As it is, it penetrates to the deepest layers of our perception of being and becomes an ontological problem for philosophical and theological consideration. What is it about the nature of time that forces it to the center of Orwell's nightmare? What is the proper theological response to this problem?

Ellul / On Technique as Sociological Desacralization

Why indeed should the technician justify himself? He feels in no way guilty; his good intentions are as clear as their excellent results are undeniable. No, the technician has no need of justification. And if ever the slightest doubt were to penetrate his consciousness, his answer would be as clear as it would be staggering: The Man for whom I am working is Humanity, the Species, the Proletariat, the Race, Man the creature, Man the eternal, even you. All technical systems, whether they be expressed in Communist or Liberal phraseology, come back in the final analysis to this abstraction. All technicians, too. The technicians, in any case, do not have sufficient intellectual curiosity to ask themselves what their favorite abstraction really means or what the relation is between this abstraction and technique. Not, one supposes, that intellectual curiosity would be worth much here. The abstraction, Man, is only an epiphenomenon in the Marxist sense; a natural secretion of technical progress.[124]

Introduction. In 1964, a book appeared in the American setting that has become a primary text for the discussion of the philosophy (and theol-

---

[122]Ibid., 36.

[123]Ibid., 176.

[124]Jacques Ellul, *The Technological Society* (New York: Alfred A. Knopf, 1976) 390.

ogy) of technology—*The Technological Society* by Jacques Ellul. Ellul advances the discussion of the central technological forces at play in Tocqueville's American democratic environment to their ultimate conclusion, namely the rise of autonomous technology. Because this book contains the fundamentals of Ellul's approach to technology and the establishment of his central argument, I will limit my discussion primarily to it. All his later work in the field presupposes this text.[125]

The original French title of this work, *La Technique ou l'enjeu du siècle* (literally, "Technique: The Stake of This Century"), betrays the significantly different connotation of the term *technique* as opposed to *technology*. Ellul defines technique as follows: "The totality of methods rationally arrived at and having absolute efficiency (for a given stage of development) in every field of human activity."[126] In Ellul, Orwell's imaginative, totalitarian political vision has become a totalitarianism of the mind, encompassing both the social and psychological realms in the real world. He believes that whereas the machine stands as the point of origin of modern technique, and itself embodies pure technique, the latter has become essentially independent of it in the modern world. Indeed, it is the task of technique to assimilate all that exists within the machine: " . . . the ideal for which technique strives is the mechanization of everything it encounters."[127] Ellul sees the growth and development of this machine-generated technique as inevitable throughout the modern world, and early in his book he concludes that "all-embracing technique is in fact the *consciousness* of the mechanized world" [my emphasis].[128] Clearly, for Ellul technique has penetrated to the deepest layers of the psyche of contemporary man, and now represents a deeper reality than, say, sexuality (Sigmund Freud) or economics (Karl Marx).

The importance of Ellul's work for the subject of American biblical hermeneutics goes beyond the material content of his philosophy of tech-

---

[125]See, for example, Ellul's more recent discussion in *The Technological System* (New York: Continuum, 1980) 1. Here he writes, "Technology is not content with *being*, or in our world, with being the *principle or determining factor*. Technology has become a system. . . . Twenty-five years ago, I arrived at the notion of the 'technological society'; but now, that stage is passed. Nevertheless, we are faced with the major problem of what makes up the specific nature of our society, its chief characteristic." Thus, Ellul understands the transition from "the technological society" to "the technological system" as one that represents the intensification of technique from being one major factor in modern life to becoming all-inclusive in all aspects. All of this presupposes the reality of technique itself and the case that Ellul makes for it in *The Technological Society*.

[126]Ellul, *Technological Society*, xxv.

[127]Ibid., 12.

[128]Ibid., 6.

nology. Ellul is a committed Christian, and he understands his work as carrying profound theological implications. Moreover, the particular way he chooses to textualize his explicit theological interests has a structural parallel to my own. James Y. Holloway gives this brief description of Ellul's own literary/theological technique.

> His sociological and political analyses are written under the demands he knows as a Christian, and it is precisely because of this commitment that he judges it dishonest as well as meaningless to introduce "Christianity" as an authority for these writings. Instead, his sociological and political analyses are a pole for his theological and biblical writings—"compositions in counterpoint," he calls them. These "compositions in counterpoint" are in no sense a Tillichian "theology of *correlation*." Rather, Ellul is composing a "theology of *confrontation*"—the biblical message written to confront the developments (especially the technical developments) in modern society. His work, he explains, has from the first turned on "the contradiction between the evolution of the modern world [notably the technical evolution] and the biblical content of revelation [author's emphasis].[129]

In Ellul's restricted sense, therefore, theology is approached dialectically in a way that appears on the surface to be similar to my own. Yet, a closer analysis shows that the similarity, while significant at one level, diverges markedly at another. Ellul and I agree that the thrust of the biblical message forces the Christian to be somewhat at odds with the modern world, whether the specific manifestation of that world be an American or another cultural context. Religion and modern secular society are simply not the same thing! Furthermore, we agree that the Christian must analyze and confront theologically the secular world as vigorously as possible. Ellul himself writes,

> I have sought to confront theological and biblical knowledge and sociological analysis without trying to come to any artificial or philosophical synthesis; instead, I try to place the two face to face, in order to shed some light on what is real socially and real spiritually. That is why I can say that the reply to each of my sociological analyses is found implicitly in a corresponding theological book, and inversely, my theology is fed on socio-political experience. But I refuse to construct a *system* of thought, or to offer up some Christian or prefabricated socio-political solutions. I want to provide Christians with the means of thinking out *for themselves* the meaning of their involvement in the modern world [author's emphasis].[130]

Yet, it is precisely the sources that Ellul chooses to clarify this confrontation that reveal much about the theological differences between us—a point as significant as the similarities. In fact, the goal of setting theolog-

---

[129]James Y. Holloway, "West of Eden," in Holloway, ed., *Introducing Jacques Ellul* (Grand Rapids MI: Eerdmans, 1970) 20.

[130]Jacques Ellul, "From Jacques Ellul," ibid., 6.

ical/biblical knowledge and sociological/political knowledge in sharpest juxtaposition has meant that Ellul has painted both these realms in rationally extracted forms that reduce them to diametrically opposed abstractions. The fact that he characteristically produces either theological/biblical books or sociological/political books, while graphically establishing the independence of each, tends to play up the confrontational element at the expense of mutual interpenetration. Such structural decisions—such techniques, I might say—have extraordinary significance in the unfolding of his intellectual program.

The heart of the difference of approaches taken by Ellul and myself lies in our understanding of the Bible and how it ought to function in the Christian context. Ellul is not guided primarily in his study of the Bible by the historical-critical method. In an article written several years after *The Technological Society* to introduce Ellul's work with the Bible to the American public, Vernard Eller gave a succinct view of his way of reading the biblical text. Eller pointed to his exegetical method as consisting of a certain understanding of inspiration.

> Central to Ellul's approach . . . is his insistence that inspiration is not a localized action affecting only the original author of a passage and that only at the moment of his writing. Inspiration by the Spirit is a continuing and cumulative activity that accompanies a text from the occurrence of the events it will later record, through the transmission and interpretation of the oral tradition; through the act of its being written down; through its consequent arrangement; supplementation and redaction; through its ultimate finding of a place in the canon; and clear on to its being pondered and understood by the believing reader.[131]

The attempt, then, is to establish an integrated method of biblical interpretation that runs from ancient events recorded in the Bible to modern readers of this record. This unity achieved by the Holy Spirit stands, naturally, in strict antipathy to the modern unifying force of technique. Ellul finds support for this holistic doctrine of inspiration within the biblical material itself. Eller describes his perspective in this way: "There is enough *historical* continuity in the process of the Bible's *formation* to justify the assumption that an *ideational* continuity might be found in its *content*" [author's emphasis].[132] Such a comprehensive view of the work of the Holy Spirit sets Ellul in obvious opposition, for example, to the historical-critical program of Rudolf Bultmann. Ellul himself writes,

> What we are proposing is obviously the direct opposite of what Bultmann has been sponsoring. Bultmann begins by affirming the given real-

---

[131]Vernard Eller, "How Jacques Ellul Reads the Bible," *Christian Century* 89 (29 November 1972): 1,213.

[132]Ibid.

ities of the world, that is, science or history, and then proceeds to criticize, not just the modes of explanation, but the very core of what is passed on to us by the Bible. When the Bible has been stripped in this way, all that finally remains is myself in relation to a God to whom I have given existence. The same applies to the attempt of Tillich to find common ground between culture and revelation. What is more clearly needed here is the either-or which is more consonant, I think, with Scripture, not the synthesis or reconciliation which each attempts with new methods and which gives no help to those who famish through appeasement and toleration.[133]

In fact, Bultmann does not understand himself as criticizing "the very core" of the Bible. Neither does Bultmann finally find himself "in relation to a God to whom I have given existence." In fact, the Scripture as such is not constructed on the basis of an either-or, as Ellul claims. Some of Scripture is, but some of Scripture is not. The biblical writers were greatly influenced by their respective surrounding cultures. They accommodated much of what they encountered in this regard, just as they also rejected much. The theological task is to determine how this was done in such a way that we can employ the Bible as guidance for the structurally similar issues of our day that lie "on the boundary." Whether one finds the specifics of Bultmann's program as positive or negative, one should not overly hastily throw out his guidance on this crucial theological point.

From the Metaphysics of Machines to Technique. As indicated above, Ellul has made a significant philosophical advancement over the previous discussion of the machine by raising it to a genuinely philosophical (and, ultimately, theological) level. It is now impossible to evaluate fully an approach to "technics," such as that advanced by Mumford, apart from some consideration of "technique." How does Ellul make this important philosophical move? As indicated above, he clearly establishes the primacy of the machine in any discussion of technique. He writes, "Technique certainly began with the machine . . . [and] without the machine the world of technique would not exist."[134] In another context, he notes that "capitalism did not create our world; the machine did."[135] In more specific historical terms, he locates the beginning of machine technique after 1750.[136] Today, however, this primal unity between machine and technique no longer exists. He continues,

> Technique has now become almost completely independent of the machine, which has lagged far behind its offspring. . . . It is the machine which

---

[133]Jacques Ellul, *The Ethics of Freedom* (Grand Rapids MI: Eerdmans, 1976) 68–69.

[134]Ibid., 3.

[135]Ibid., 5.

[136]Ibid., 111.

is now entirely dependent upon technique, and the machine represents only a small part of technique. . . . [Indeed,] the machine is now not even the most important aspect of technique (though it is perhaps the most spectacular); technique has taken over all of man's activities, not just his productive activity.[137]

It is crucial, then, to understand that Ellul's position that technique has become totally autonomous in our society begins with this break from the machine, which gave it birth. He describes in further detail how the dominance of technique has taken place. "Technique has enough of the mechanical in its nature to enable it to cope with the machine, but it surpasses and transcends the machine because it remains in close touch with the human order. The metal monster could not go on forever torturing mankind. It found in technique a rule as hard and inflexible as itself."[138] The material divergence in the positions of Ellul and Mumford begins to arise with this characterization of the machine as "the metal monster." Faced with the inextricable reality of the machine that was essentially inhuman, technique arose in society to adapt it to human realities. Because this rational enterprise worked so well with reference to the machine, it increasingly began to be applied as an integrative force to all other aspects of society as well. In short, for Ellul, humans have become "the object of technique and the offspring of the mating of man and machine."[139] It is at this point that the genuinely philosophical and theological perspectives of technique emerge, including its relevance, as a result, for American biblical hermeneutics.

Just as Marx argued that the proletariat class had been created by the industrialization brought about by the bourgeois, Ellul develops his thesis that the machine created technique in the vacuum created by its own inherent inhumanness.

> Technique integrates everything. It avoids shock and sensational events. Man is not adapted to a world of steel; technique adapts him to it. It changes the arrangement of this blind world so that man can be a part of it without colliding with its rough edges, without the anguish of being delivered up to the inhuman. Technique thus provides a model; it specifies attitudes that are valid once and for all. *The anxiety aroused in man by the turbulence of the machine is soothed by the consoling hum of a unified society* [my emphasis].[140]

Ellul, in essential agreement with Mumford, understands the impact of the machine on human existence to have been of such essential importance that it fundamentally altered our way of being in the world. The

---

[137]Ibid., 4.

[138]Ibid.

[139]Ibid., 146.

[140]Ibid., 6.

machine broke down whatever primal vestiges of unity existed between humanity and world.[141] And, because humans cannot live for long in such a chaotic environment, technique arose as a way of reintegrating them into their environment. Better the ordered existence of the slave than the disorientation of lost order itself. In a powerful statement that manifests the essence of Ellul's view of the machine, he writes,

> Admittedly, the machine has enriched man as it has changed him. The machine's senses and organs have multiplied the powers of human senses and organs, enabling man to penetrate a new milieu and revealing to him unknown sights, liberties, and servitudes. *He has been liberated little by little from physical constraints, but he is all the more the slave of abstract ones.* He acts through intermediaries and consequently has lost contact with reality. . . . He no longer knows wood or iron or wool. He is acquainted only with the machine. His capacity to become a mechanic has replaced his knowledge of his material; this development has occasioned profound mental and psychic transformations which cannot be assessed [my emphasis].[142]

The liberation of the machine has, therefore, resulted in the slavery of abstraction. Humans have lost their primary associations with the marrow of life. As a result, nothing in human existence, including religion, is the same anymore.

At a particular place in his book, Ellul explicitly attacks Mumford on the inability of the latter to come to terms with the autonomy of technique vis-à-vis machines. Mumford had portrayed the various modes of exploiting energy (first hydraulic energy, then coal, and finally electricity) as "the key to the evolution of technique and the moving force behind its transformations." Ellul notes, "Mumford's thesis is incomprehensible unless *technique* is restricted to the *machine*; Mumford actually makes this identification. His distinction is then valid as a plan for the historical study of machines, but it is totally invalid for the study of technical civilization. When technical civilization is considered as a whole, this classification and

---

[141]In an article in which Ellul studies the first chapters of Genesis, he summarizes his theological position on technique and the Fall: "I did not say that technique is a fruit of sin. I did not say that technique is contrary to the will of God. I did not say that technique in itself is evil. I said only that technique is not a prologation of the Edenic creation, that it is not a compliance of man to a vocation which was given to him by God, that it is not the fruit of the first nature of Adam. It is the product of the situation in which sin has put man; it is inscribed exclusively in the fallen world; it is uniquely part of this fallen world; it is a product of necessity and not of human freedom." See "Technique and the Opening Chapters of Genesis," in Carl Mitcham and Jim Grote, eds., *Theology and Technology* (Lanham MD, New York, London: University Press of America, 1984) 135. Thus, Ellul understands Adam as having a relationship of *human necessity* to the world after the Fall.

[142]Ellul, *Ethics of Freedom*, 325.

explanation are shockingly summary and superficial."[143] It is this super-ficiality that Ellul intends to correct. Later in the book, he gives a specific instance of Mumford's inability to extrapolate conceptuality from ma-chine to technique when the latter "contrasts the grandeur of the printing press with the horridness of the newspaper." He first quotes Mumford, and then critiques him.

> [Mumford writes:] "On the one side there is the gigantic printing press, a miracle of fine articulation. . . . On the other the content of the papers themselves recording the most vulgar and elementary emotional states. . . . There the impersonal, the co-operative, the objective; here the limited, the subjective, the recalcitrant, the ego, violent and full of hate and fear, etc. . . ." *Unfortunately, it did not occur to Mumford to ask whether the content of our newspapers is not really necessitated by the social form imposed on man by the ma-chine.* This content is not the product of chance or of some economic form. It is the result of precise psychological and psychoanalytical techniques. These techniques have as their goal the bringing to the individual of that which is indispensable for his satisfaction in the conditions in which the machine has placed him, of inhibiting in him the sense of revolution, of subjugating him by flattering him. In other words, journalistic content is a technical complex expressly intended to adapt the man to the machine [my emphasis].[144]

Here we see a specific payoff that results from Ellul's more metaphysical analysis of technique. The role of journalism is to adapt humans to the machine. The validity of his entire argument rides upon the question of how accurately he portrays the reality of such contemporary occupations as this one.

Ellul maintains that the machine knows no cultural, or material, bounds. This position is a natural outgrowth of his argument that I have given to this point. The machine and the principles upon which it oper-ates are universal. Therefore, technique, spawned as it is by the machine, logically shares this universal aspect. Furthermore, he believes that "technique has become objective and is transmitted *like a physical thing*; it leads thereby to a certain unity of civilization, regardless of the environ-ment or the country in which it operates" [my emphasis].[145] This char-acterization of technique as "like a physical thing" posits technique as a reality transcending culture itself. While his description here is "pre-eco-logical," it is nevertheless important to note the extreme lengths to which Ellul will go in describing the force of modern technique.

> It destroys, eliminates, or subordinates the natural world, and does not

---

[143]Ibid., 42.

[144]Ibid., 95–96.

[145]Ibid., 78.

allow this world to restore itself or even to enter into a symbiotic relation with it. The two worlds obey different imperatives, different directives, and different laws which have nothing in common. Just as hydroelectric installations take waterfalls and lead them into conduits, so the technical milieu absorbs the natural. We are rapidly approaching the time when there will be no longer any natural environment at all.[146]

Technique, therefore, stands as the new ground of human existence that is fundamentally one and the same everywhere. Its consists of two essential characteristics that are abstracted from each culture with which it comes into contact, and to which each culture is ultimately directed: (1) an acute *rationality*, "best exemplified in systematization, division of labor, creation of standards, production norms, and the like," and (2) *artificiality*. Beyond these essential characteristics, Ellul finds lesser known ones, including "technical automatism ('the one best way'), self-augmentation (technical progress is irreversible, and it progresses geometrically), monism, universalism, and autonomy."[147] The vitality of these characteristics mean that neither nature nor traditional culture is able to stand up to the force of technique.

From the standpoint of the perspective of this book, the most important of them is the *autonomous* nature of technique. If technique is truly autonomous, then, by definition, it must stand in opposition to the religion of the Bible. Furthermore, if those of us who read the Bible are situated in a culture that is fundamentally determined by autonomous technique, then the ramifications must be severe in the way that we are reading it. For Ellul, it is clear that technique has replaced traditional culture, or has become culture itself. As a result, it necessarily forces a rethinking of the way we conceive of the ground rules of modern life. If all this sounds like a new religion in its own right, then that is precisely the message Ellul wishes to bring to us.

Christianity and the Myth of Man. Ellul interprets autonomous technique as the religion of our day in the sense that it has taken over, or overtaken, the traditional ideas and function of morality. In an extended description of this phenomenon, he writes,

> Technical autonomy is apparent in respect to morality and spiritual values. . . . Morality judges moral problems; as far as technical problems are concerned, it has nothing to say. Only technical criteria are relevant. . . . Thus, technique theoretically and systematically assures to itself that liberty which it has been able to win practically. Since it has put itself beyond good and evil, it need fear no limitation whatever. It was long claimed that technique was neutral. Today this is no longer a useful distinction. . . . The power and autonomy of technique are so well secured that it, in its turn,

---

[146]Ibid., 79.

[147]Ibid.

has become the judge of what is moral, the creator of a new morality. Thus, it plays the role of creator of a new civilization as well. This morality—internal to technique—is assured of not having to suffer from technique. In any case, in respect to traditional morality, technique affirms itself as an independent power. Man alone is subject, it would seem, to moral judgment. We no longer live in that primitive epoch in which things were good or bad in themselves. Technique in itself is neither, and can therefore do what it will. It is truly autonomous.[148]

Thus, for Ellul, technique has escaped the strictures of morality and traditional values, by creating a new arena for its own activity. In this sense, technique is *not* a direct attack upon the traditional values of our cultural heritage. If it were, it would doubtlessly be attacked as an enemy by the guardians of that heritage. This creative force is what allows technique to assume an autonomous reality as it continues to extend its power in our lives. The result is that many interpreters frame the problem in the wrong way: the central point is not really the problem of the neutrality of technique (it can be used for good or evil), rather it is the fact that technique renders *our* traditional values neutral (our perception of good and evil is no longer meaningful). Technical solutions to problems have replaced moral solutions. As indicated above, this new creative force in the world was spawned by the machine. Just as the machine opened up a new realm that was discontinuous with all which had preceded it, so too is the child of the machine, technique. Like Mumford, Ellul argues that the attempt to relate to this new realm with the old philosophical (and theological) perspectives is to ensure our capitulation before its creative force. The problem lies, therefore, in the fact that those grounded in traditional morality underestimate the magnitude of the creative power of autonomous technique.

Technique as a creative force is the key to Ellul's interpretation of it as a modern religion. In relation to traditional religion, the specific point that it asserts itself is at that aspect of existence we conventionally term the sacred, the spiritual, or the mysterious. Thus, although "man cannot live without a sense of the secret,"[149] autonomous technique works counter to it.

> The invasion of technique desacralizes the world in which man is called upon to live. For technique nothing is sacred, there is no mystery, no taboo. . . . Technique worships nothing, respects nothing. It has a single role: to strip off externals, to bring everything to light, and by rational use to transform everything into means. More than science, which limits itself to explaining the "how," technique desacralizes because it demonstrates (by evidence and not by reason, through use and not through books) that

---

[148]Ibid., 134.

[149]Ibid., 142.

mystery does not exist. Science brings to the light of day everything man had believed sacred. Technique takes possession of it and enslaves it. The sacred cannot resist. . . . The mysterious is merely that which has not yet been technicized.[150]

Autonomous technique does not explain away the mysterious; it creates something new that reveals the mysterious to be unreal. If something exists outside the technical realm that claims human attention, then it is assailed by technique. By its very nature, technique cannot allow the independent existence of anything other than itself. Its creative force takes possession of everything it encounters—religion being no exception to this rule. But, because humans cannot live without a sense of the sacred, they follow the next logical course of action, they transfer their "sense of the sacred to the very thing which has destroyed its former object: to technique itself."[151] It is with the convergence of these two powerful forces—the human necessity for the sacred, and the autonomous creative power of technique—that Ellul lays the intellectual framework for theologically addressing technology. What, then, is the theological track record of the church for this technological challenge?

The answer to this question is to be framed in the larger one of the Christian role itself in technological development. Historically, the issue is clear-cut. Since technique rose to dominance first in the "Christian West," must not this religious tradition assume much of the blame of bringing to reality the harbinger of its own demise? Ellul finds that the answer is no, once the historical evidence has been properly analyzed. As Christianity rose to dominance in the Roman Empire, for example, he approvingly notes the decline of Roman organization. He maintains, therefore, that "it is not a coincidence that Rome declined as Christianity triumphed. The Emperor Julian was certainly justified in accusing the Christians of ruining the industry of the Empire."[152] This nontechnological character of pure Christianity is evident in Christian centuries subsequent to the breakup of the Roman empire. Thus, "the society which developed from the tenth to the fourteenth century was vital, coherent, and unanimous; but it was characterized by a total absence of the technical will. It was a-capitalistic as well as a-technical."[153] It is true that "very feebly a technical movement" began to take shape already in the twelfth century, but this "developed under the influence of the East."[154] Therefore, he maintains that "the technical impetus of our civilization came from

---

[150]Ibid.

[151]Ibid., 143.

[152]Ibid., 34.

[153]Ibid.

[154]Ibid.

the East, at first through the intermediacy of the Judaei (a particular kind of trader) and the Venetians, and later through the Crusades."[155] In this way, the following conclusion is established: *"The technical movement of the West developed in a world which had already withdrawn from the dominant influence of Christianity"* [my emphasis].[156] Therefore, Christianity cannot be held accountable for the general course of Western civilization that has resulted in the dominance of technique.

Besides the chronological one of historical development, Ellul notes that two additional arguments have customarily been given for the theological point of view that Christianity "paved the way for technical development"[157]: (1) It suppressed slavery, an institution that held technique in check, and (2) it secularized nature, thereby giving rise to technique. Ellul disagrees with both of these conclusions. Concerning the first, he finds that "there was in fact greater technical progress in civilizations where slavery was prevalent (for example, Egypt) than in others where that institution was practically unknown (for example, Israel)."[158] Therefore, he finds no absolute relationship between technique and the absence of slavery. Second, he maintains that the association of secularized nature (which Christianity did, in fact, bring about) and the rise of technique is specious. Rather than promoting technique, a desacralized view of nature inhibits the natural tendency toward a form of proto-technique itself: magic. Christianity, therefore, deprived man of the natural "powers, or gods of nature which man could put at the service of technique." In all instances, therefore, Christianity is exonerated historically as a force in the development of the technique of the East. Rather than aiding the development of technique, Christians consistently asked the moral question that came from outside technique itself, "Is it righteous?" Once a particular technique was considered righteous "from *every* point of view, it was adopted, but even then with excessive caution."[159] In this way, Ellul concludes, "The search for justice before God, the measuring of technique by other criteria than those of technique itself—these were the great obstacles that Christianity opposed to technical progress. They operated in the Middle Ages in all areas of life, and made history coincide with theology."[160] Once the true historical record is known and Christianity is seen as a obstacle to technical progress, rather than an agent of it, the major question looms as to how faithfully modern Christianity has adhered to

---

[155]Ibid., 35.

[156]Ibid.

[157]Ibid.

[158]Ibid., 36.

[159]Ibid., 37.

[160]Ibid., 38.

its own traditional critique of technique.

In general, Ellul is unforgiving in his criticism of Christianity in the modern West. The few prophetic voices, such as that raised by Søren Kierkegaard, were to no avail: "In the middle of the nineteenth century, when technique had hardly begun to develop, another voice was raised in prophetic warning against it. The voice was Kierkegaard's. But his warnings, solidly thought out though they were, and in the strongest sense of the word prophetic, were not heeded. . . . They were too close to the truth."[161] The church had already adapted itself too closely to the rise of technique, especially in the more advanced industrialized nations. Witness the primary instance of this in England, where the Puritans "even after their political failure, were the predominant influence."[162] Ellul sees them as having "exploded all prevailing religious taboos and developed a practical and utilitarian mentality that emphasized the use and even the exploitation of the good things of this world given by God to men."[163] The Church of England itself had adapted "a kind of secularization of religion." For it, "religion is no longer the framework of society; it can no longer impose its taboos or forms upon it. Rather, it integrates itself into society, adjusts to it, and adopts the notion of social utility as criterion and justification."[164] The result of the loss of the religious framework of society was the rise of a certain plasticity that came to characterize other societies after the English experience, for example, France and America. In France, the monarchy took the leadership role in advancing technique through the propagation of scientific academies and institutes. The American setting itself benefited enormously from the entire European experience, especially this new social plasticity that the demise of Christianity brought forth.

> In the United States [the convergence of the state and private technical interests] took place at the beginning of the nineteenth century. Until then, the society of this country was inorganic. But at that time the American social milieu was favorable; moreover, the Americans profited from the technical consciousness evolved in Europe, and so they arrived immediately at a model for technique. [Siegfried] Giedion has noted that the Americans began by mechanizing complex operations, which produced the assembly line, whereas the Europeans tended to mechanize simple operations, such as spinning. This American accomplishment was the result of the exceptional flexibility of the American milieu.[165]

---

[161]Ibid., 55.

[162]Ibid., 56.

[163]Ibid.

[164]Ibid., 156.

[165]Ibid., 58–59.

The result is that Americans, who must have some sort of ordering principle in their society like everyone else, instigated something to substitute for the Christian church and the monarchy. In particular, the fluidity of democratic America liberated the way for the free, intense, and relatively unhindered development of technique. The new religion of technique would develop in this cultural ethos most intensely of all, with the Myth of Man as its centerpiece.[166]

Chronological Abstractions. Based on our discussion thus far, it comes as no surprise that Ellul argues that technique has penetrated the "deepest recesses of the human being."[167] This has been accomplished by the way in which it has modified the entire environment in which human existence now takes place. This environment includes "everything that goes to make up his milieu, his livelihood, habitat, and habits."[168] But this modification extends beyond such practical considerations, and includes the more abstract realms of space and time. His discussion of space centers around the loss of *Lebensraum* brought about by the effects of the increased technologization of life. In terms of the problem of time, he finds Mumford's discussion of the centrality of the clock in the technical society to be precisely on target. While the discussion of time does not seem to play as central a role in Ellul's text as it does in Mumford's, Ellul clearly presupposes the work of the latter on this problem. "Today the human being is dissociated from the essence of life; instead of *living* time, he is split up and parceled out by it. Lewis Mumford is right in calling the clock the most important machine of our culture. And he is right too in asserting that the clock has made modern progress and efficiency possible through its rapidity of action and the co-ordination it effects in man's daily activities."[169] The clock, therefore, is the machine par excellence that adapted humans to all other machines. Ellul dates this split of abstract time from lived time during the sixteenth century with the introduction of private clocks.

> Thenceforward, time was an abstract measure separated from the traditional rhythms of life and nature. It became mere quantity. But since life is inseparable from time, life too was forced to submit to the new guiding principle. From then on, life itself was measured by the machine; its organic functions obeyed the mechanical. Eating, working, and sleeping were at the beck and call of machinery. Time, which had been the measure of organic sequences, was broken and dissociated. Human life ceased to be an ensemble, a whole, and became a disconnected set of activities having

---

[166]Ibid., 390.

[167]Ibid., 325.

[168]Ibid., 326.

[169]Ibid., 156.

no other bond than the fact that they were performed by the same individual. Mechanical abstraction and rigidity permeated the whole structure of being.

The real importance of this text lies in the way it posits the clock as the fundamental means whereby individual humans are disassociated from organic, physical processes. Human adaptation to the machine, in other words, could only take place once the primal unity with nature was severed. The human body was the final stronghold of resistance that fought the penetration of the machine into the center of human consciousness; the clock was the instrument of abstraction designed to overcome this resistance.

The quantification of time brought on by the clock, and its effect on the mechanization of the individual, has a strong parallel in Ellul's analysis of the "massification" of society.[170] He finds that Jean-Paul Sartre's remark that "statistics can never be dialectics" is the key insight at this point. The following analysis of the nondialectical character of statistics drives home this point.

> There is an opposition (even a mutual exclusion) between statistics and dialectics. They differ not merely in their mode of explaining but also in their very mode of apprehending the world and action. Statistics is necessarily a univocal method that expresses an aspect of reality which is uncombinable with any other (except other statistics). . . . Statistics (and every technique) can proceed only by affirmation, by exclusion of negations, refusal, and destruction.[171]

This discussion is important, not only as a background for the massification Orwell portrays in 1984, but for an understanding of the *intrinsic* antipathy between biblical dialectics and modern society. To this end, Ellul finds "a fixed connection between statistics and the economics of mass society." I might say that Ellul considers statistics, and the use that is put to them by the techniques of propaganda, to be the grammar of modern societal existence. It brings an analogous sort of language of quantification to society, as does the clock, which proceeds by the abstraction of time. Statistics are utilized in the modern world as a way of imposing a restricted, one-way view of reality. If truth is relational in nature, then truth has no opportunity for manifestation in a society that is grounded in statistics.

The issue of technique in relation to democracy and totalitarianism is a natural unfolding of all that has been said about Ellul's discussion of "the technological society." Politically, he stands as an advocate of liberal democracy. But, he finds technique an opponent of both liberalism and democracy, as well as true Christianity. In particular, he considers technique to be the "boundary of democracy," noting that "what technique wins,

---

[170]Ibid., 206–208.

[171]Ibid., 206.

democracy loses."[172] By utilizing the machine as a simile, he is able to speak of a propaganda machine in modern "so-called" democratic societies that "*must* become more and more intense in order to dominate its rivals" [author's emphasis].[173] The heart of the problem modern democracy faced, and which ultimately brought about its reduction to the technical state, is the rapid development of the machine in the military context. Here, Ellul observes that no matter what grand theories of war and strategic doctrines evolved, "one factor always upsets everything: the machine." He finds himself in agreement, therefore, with the position that "the techniques of modern war have destroyed democracy." In the new age of technique, the traditional break on technical progress that is embodied in parliamentary government is considered as "excess baggage." Democratic institutions are too "ponderous and slow." He continues, ". . . technical advance gradually invades the state, which in turn is compelled to assume forms and adopt institutions favorable to this advance."[174] In this environment, all questions are reduced to the one of the efficiency of the machine. Only the technician can make the proper determination at this point, not the common citizen, not even the well-informed citizen. The role of the democratic state is reduced analogously to that of the individual who has been replaced by the automatic machine: this person "retains no function except that of inspecting the machine and seeing that it remains in working order." As a result, Ellul sees democracy in the modern world as being reduced to an "old-fashioned republican mask." What has emerged in its place is political totalitarianism. Whether that totalitarianism be couched economically in capitalistic or communistic terms is of secondary importance.

The specific opening in the technological society by which totalitarianism found its way into the political system is located in the problem of the coordination of the multiplicity of techniques that have emerged in the modern world. No other single institution is comprehensive enough to bring about the desired effect: "Thus, the techniques of the state—military, police, administrative, and political—made their appearance."[175] In such an environment, the individual *as individual* becomes an enemy. To this point, Ellul concludes,

> The individual is not by himself rational enough to accept what is necessary to the machines. He rebels too easily. He requires an agency to constrain him, and the state had to play this role—but the state now could not be the incoherent, powerless, and arbitrary state of tradition. It had to be

---

[172]Ibid., 209.

[173]Ibid., 276.

[174]Ibid., 278.

[175]Ibid., 115.

an effective state, equal to the functioning of the economic regime and in control of everything, to the end that machines which had developed at random should become "coherent."

Thus, for Ellul, the control of the individual is rooted in the control of the individual for the sake of efficiency. In fact, he understands precisely this benign appearance of technique as a signal of its greatest danger. Speaking of the effect of technique on the diversity of civilizations still remaining in the world, Ellul writes, "Behind this diversity is to be noted an absolute incompatibility between the technical type of civilization and all the others. Technicians have not willed this outcome; no one seeks consciously to destroy a civilization. This is simply the proverbial collision between the earthenware pot and the iron pot. What happens, happens, despite the best possible intentions of the iron pot."[176] The technician, armed with the best of intentions, becomes the great destroyer of traditional culture, values, and religion. Behind the technician stands the machine, and Ellul finds that "only madness is inaccessible to the machine."[177] We have, indeed, come full circle from the promises and dangers of the new democratic age that Tocqueville heralded more than a hundred years earlier. Yet, the embryonic misgivings inherent in this age as seen by Tocqueville, appear more than justified in the Ellulian world.

• Conclusion •

Human beings are technical creatures, whether living in biblical times or in our own. That is, they must employ various means to construct their lives, even religious lives, if they are to find meaning in life. Unlike other members of the animal kingdom, their lives are not prescribed in advance, either materially or spiritually. The insights of the Spanish existentialist José Ortega y Gasset in his "Reflections on Technique" (1939) retain their power today.[178] But the necessary use of some technique is not to be identified with the use of that particular technological system presented by modern technology. The techniques by which humans reshape the created world and human existence are immensely varied. Because of the pervasiveness of the modern technological system characterized, in Ellul's description, by unification, autonomy, speed, ef-

---

[176]Ibid., 124.

[177]Ibid., 404.

[178]José Ortega y Gasset, *History as a System* (New York: Norton, 1961), contains an essay entitled "Man the Technician." A newer, revised translation by Helene Weyl, with revisions by Edwin Williams, appears under the title "Thoughts on Technology," in C. Mitcham and R. Mackey, eds., *Philosophy and Technology: Readings* (New York: Free Press, 1972) 290–313.

ficiency, monism, and the like, it is necessary for theology to inquire into the basic character of that alternative technique exhibited in the Bible in order to regain a critical posture over against it.

This study of the preceding texts reveals the primacy of the technology problem for the study of American ethos. They bespeak an emerging technological consciousness that is increasingly difficult to separate from that of the remainder of the world. America seems distinguishable from the Western cultural sphere only by virtue of the way the excesses of that general culture are left to develop unimpeded. America, conceived as an experiment in human nature, was to become more modestly the frontier of Western cultural imperialism. It is my thesis that a primary way to evaluate theologically this more problematic American ethos is by means of the category of time. As we have seen, time is fundamental to the interior consciousness of democratic technology, and, so our theological tradition informs us, it lies at the heart of the biblical message as well. This thesis has the correlative aspect that the many divisions in biblical Christianity are more the result of our inability to develop a common understanding of our own ethos as readers than the lack of a unified biblical theology. Specifically, I have argued that this major vein of American ethos assumes a trajectory of thought that is nurtured in a substratum of democratic consciousness, continues as a disruptive force in the machine, and evolves as the emergence of pure rationalistic technique that tends toward the systematization and control of all aspects of the modern world. The problem now becomes the specific determination of the use we can make of this critical perspective of our own culture for the task of biblical interpretation.

The texts that we have examined profoundly engage the central problematics of American ethos. A culture must find adequate means of social cohesion based on self-legitimation. As an emerging nation, America experienced this problem in a particularly acute form. Who was this new people? What was the meaning of the past experiences that had brought its divergent population together? What common goals and aspirations could be forged out of the diversity of previous experiences? I have already argued that this conceptuality is really a way of *timing space*, in the sense that America becomes a geographical locality infused with a particular hermeneutics of time serving as an ideological legitimation of the new cultural identity. The idea of a perpetual newness has been a part of this ideological framework of the American experience from the beginning: sometimes taken in a religious sense, sometimes not.

In his provocative little book *The Republic of Technology*, Daniel J. Boorstin notes the American tendency to embody features very similar to Orwellian totalitarianism: lack of differentiation and the rule of the present. Concerning the former, he writes, "The supreme law of the Republic of Technology is convergence, the tendency for everything to become more like everything else." He understands those problems that divide humanity (tribalism, racism, "the crusading spirit in religion," and the like) to be only temporary barriers to the converging powers of technology "which will eventually triumph." Ironically, however, egalitarian forces in American society only create new ways of separating people. Technological products become so pervasive that as our sight and vision in space becomes increasingly enlarged, we seem somehow to become imprisoned in the present. "The electronic technology that reaches out instantaneously over the continents does very little to help us cross the centuries."[179]

Throughout our discussion of Mumford, Orwell, and Ellul, we find a chorus of voices that effectively function as a commentary on Tocqueville's critique of democracy and embody an intensifying level of concern for the uncritical way time is mechanized at the interior of our ethnic consciousness. Whether America be defined in terms of pure democracy and its perpetual cult of the new, the mechanical abstractions of disembodied time brought about by the machine, or the land of the quantification and massification of life made possible by the clock, the warnings imaginatively portrayed by our cultural interpreters persistently accompany the American experiment from its democratic beginnings. The point is simply this: the more we abstract ourselves from the natural world and lose a sense of commonality of purpose and destiny with it, the more subject we become to our own tyrannical potentialities. None of our authors maintain that the answer to the complex problems facing American culture lies in simply giving ourselves over to nature, or returning to a romantic past. The technology that has grown so pervasively from the seedbed of our democratic form has brought the special American experience into the mainstream of the universal questions of human existence. The question is, how do we shape this environment we have inherited in order to enter into a more meaningful existence? With that basic question in mind, let us turn to a consideration of sacred texts.

---

[179]Boorstin, *Republic of Technology*, 5.

TEXTs:
Sacred Texts

• Introduction •

The trajectory of American ethos that runs from democratic consciousness, through the machine and machinelike societal structures, to the modern emergence of oppressive technique, requires an adequate Judeo-Christian response. As I have indicated previously, one of the fundamental ways that American biblical hermeneutics distinguishes itself from either descriptive analyses of the history of biblical interpretation in America, or prescriptive statements that address American culture from a biblical standpoint, is its positioning of these independent realities in dialectical relationship. Because the intention is primarily theological, methodologically the procedure is to feed the formative features of American culture into the center of the interpretive process in order to insure a vital theology that is intimately involved with the public world and one that makes a difference there.

The central text that portrays the general biblical orientation to the problem of time and its human relevance is the so-called Primeval History in Genesis 1–11. These are texts that narrate the broad context of the human condition that stands as presupposition behind the specificities of Judaic religious practice. Literary-critical scholars have for generations approached these texts from the standpoint of the analysis of the J and P sources. This approach has revealed certain insights into the composition and meaning of this material. Literary criticism is a provocative method of biblical criticism serving the purposes and intentions of the scientific mentality, which is interested in such problems as the origin and history of the construction of the text. Through decades of work, although the results of specific interpretations are disputed, our knowledge of the process of composition of the Primeval History has been greatly enriched by this approach. Recently, however, interest has been shown in interpreting them in terms of the unified structure found in the present textual construction.[1] This holistic approach corresponds better to the overall intention of hermeneutics, which always places the perspective of meaning

---

[1]Cf., for example, Gordon J. Wenham, "The Coherence of the Flood Narrative," *Vetus Testamentum* 28:3 (July 1978): 336–48. Frank Cross writes, "While aware of two levels, and not infrequently more than two levels, in JE tradition, we are less inclined to resort to the multiplication of 'documents' and more inclined to speak generally of the 'Epic sources' or simply 'Epic tradition.' " In Cross, *Canaanite Myth and Hebrew Epic* (Cambridge MA: Harvard University Press, 1973) 293.

at the forefront of interpretation, thereby emphasizing the reality of the present text.[2] From this holistic, hermeneutical perspective, therefore, the analysis of historical criticism functions most profoundly in a negative way. It informs us what we *cannot* say about the meaning of the text. Thus, while it is superfluous merely to restate the historical-critical conclusions of biblical exegesis in the context of American biblical hermeneutics, awareness of them is presupposed and we would err in violating the insights that the application of these methodologies offer us. Important to remember here is that the goal of American biblical hermeneutics is to make an earnest contribution to Christian theology, and biblical thought arguably has been rendered ineffective by many of its most recent interpreters because of their atomizing interpretive tendencies. The Bible, as object, increasingly becomes viewed as just another cultural resource to be drawn upon and manipulated as other ideological supports according to the whims of the people. The result is that the Bible is rendered ineffective according to its own critical intentionality precisely at that point where the secular culture increasingly finds the means of building its own supports.

In the history of Christian exegesis, the textual power of the Primeval History itself has been mollified by reading it as a kind of prologue to the major body of the Hebrew Scriptures. From the standpoint of this body of literature, the religion of Israel (and hence, by extension, Christianity) is said to begin in Genesis 12 with the Call of Abraham by Yahweh.[3] In response to this call, Abraham is considered to be the first believer in Yahweh to walk upon the stage of human history. The Call of Abraham initiates, in other words, a new kind of history that leads eventually to the appearance of Jesus as the Christ. In this way, Genesis 1–11, which deals with the progenitors of the human race and not simply the Jews, serves as the background for the historical religion of the Israelites. Interestingly, the Hebrew text does not make the same neat distinction between prehistory and history as does the tradition of Old Testament exegesis. In fact, Genesis 12:1 begins with a waw-consecutive, indicating an explicit continuity between what precedes and that which follows in the Abrahamic narrative. Furthermore, no stylistic device is inserted at this point to indicate the beginning of a major new unit. A silent partner in the history of this exegesis undoubtedly is the predisposition toward the historical appearance of Jesus the Christ that has accompanied the

---

[2]One can seek the hermeneutical implications of each strand of the various literary sources, of course, but this in no way minimizes the priority of the present text in the interpretive process.

[3]This is not intended as a historical statement. Historically, Moses would be considered the founder of Yahwism. This faith then co-opts the original religion of Abraham and utilizes it by transformation into patriarchal Yahwism.

Christian reading of the Hebrew Scriptures. Because of the Christian prejudice of relegating these writings to the historical past (chronology) in order to utilize them as a legitimation of Jesus (promise), those parts of the Hebrew Bible that tend to fall outside history receive a secondary position in the interpretive process. In a way reminiscent of American theologians engaged in the common American practice of "timing space" described below, the Christian tradition adopted the strategy of timing the cultural space between the writings of the two Testaments by the chronological designation Old/New. (I discuss this in more detail below.) The consequences in this form of playing down the Hebrew Scriptures in Christian theology have been enormous.[4] Furthermore, since this designation was meant to be all inclusive, those writings that fell under the rubric of old (that is, were a part of the Hebrew Scriptures), and yet were not time-oriented in and of themselves, fell in stature to a place of less importance. In this way of reasoning, the Primeval History was of secondary importance, because it prepared the historical path for the advent of Jesus as the Promised One only in a very distant sense, or by means of highly speculative typological exegesis. Genesis 1–11 might well give us some crucial details about the universal human condition (for example, the entrance of sin through Adam's Fall), but the history of salvation that initiated the process of the advent of Jesus began with the Call of Abraham. Genesis 1–11 remained as a crucial substructure for this history, but it exists as substructure or prologue all the same, in spite of the textual evidence that it ought to be read as a narrative piece with Genesis 12 and following.

Once Genesis 1–11 is given its full significance in the overall intentionality of the Hebrew Scriptures, Christian theology is further enriched. Most important, the modern theological distinction between primordial history, and history as we know it, becomes less compelling. We are forced to recognize that the very distinction of primordial history/ real history is one that is also grounded in a false metaphysics of spatialized time. This false metaphysics enables the material concerns of Gen-

---

[4]My teacher, Rolf Knierim, has been one who has argued consistently against the deprecation of the Hebrew Bible by Christians. For example, he writes, "The claim that the Old Testament is theologically significant only when it is read in light of the New Testament, or of Christ, has imperialistic implications and is theologically counterproductive: it is imperialistic because it censures the Old Testament's theological validity by external criteria; and it is counterproductive because the theological significance of Christ or the New Testament, in as much [sic] as the Old Testament has something to do with them, cannot be substantiated with reference to the Old Testament's theological insignificance." In *Horizons in Biblical Theology* 6:1 (June 1984): 52. To my knowledge, Knierim has not, however, discussed the specific way that the chronological term *old* has specifically contributed to the Christian deprecation of the Hebrew Bible.

esis 1–11 to become located outside the pale of primary Christian significance. What this distinction really implies is that the primordial history conceives of a different understanding of time than the contemporary sequential view: a distinction that does not exist in the text. In primordial history, days are not necessarily twenty-four hours *long*, weeks seven days in *length*, and the like (note the spatialized terminology used to describe time), as they are in our time. As far as the Hebrew narrative is concerned, Adam and Noah are not any less authentic personages than Abraham and Jacob. The effect of placing the former in an earlier chronological frame of reference (which we may term *mythological*) is to domesticate this material under a preconceived framework and render it theologically impotent. On the other hand, the integration of Genesis 1–11 into the narratives that follow serves the purpose of uniting the history of Israel with the primordial events narrated in Genesis 1–11 under one conceptual framework. This is a matter of extreme significance in the task of biblical exegesis and theology. At this point, American biblical hermeneutics can play a central role in the interpretive process.

One of the more subtle reasons Genesis 1–11 is typically given a secondary role in Christian thought compared to the religious history that begins with the Call of Abraham is its limited size or textual space. While this fact may seem overly simplistic, the effect can be far-reaching in a technological age that values quantity and efficiency. Certainly throughout Genesis 1–11, what must be considered monumental events are given the briefest span of attention: the Creation itself, for example, only takes two chapters! Certainly, in quantifiable terms, if this material were of primary significance to Yahwism (and Christianity derivatively), more space would have been given it. Such an argument constructed on the basis of the number of words does not, however, take into consideration the important extraneous question of how this text was generated, understood, and utilized in ancient Israel. If Genesis 1, for example, served the purposes of the Hebrew cult on a regular, repetitive basis, then its dense economical style (reflecting well-worn usage and refinement) might be an indication of its vitality in the life of Israel, rather than its unimportance. In the case of such cultic usage, brevity would be an indication of primary significance, rather than secondary. Part of the hermeneutical task, therefore, is to move beyond the religion of Old Testament texts as such and to see them in relation to the religious and cultural environment that nurtured them and helped determine their specific shape. It is only when we read the Bible out of the consciousness of our own cultural concerns, and engage the biblical text at the level of its cultural relations and our own, that we can speak of a hermeneutical Bible. A hermeneutical approach to biblical interpretation such as this would always include those aspects of textual interpretation that historical criticism can provide for us. In fact, the literary analysis of the stylistic features of Genesis 1 has pointed to this kind of cultic environment for the Israelite life that nurtured this text and eventually posited it at the beginning of the Hebrew Bible.

An exegetical study of the Bible that is hermeneutical offers us the possibility of coming to terms with the biblicism that has accompanied the rise of technique in modern American life. In a biblical interpretation that seeks the full meaning of a passage, the interior meaning that accompanies the text is just as important to construct as the explicit meaning conveyed in its words. Beyond the explicit meaning of the text, tracings of this interior meaning are invariably present as well. The effect of this silent, subterranean meaning may be more important in understanding the deeper levels of textual meaning than the more readily available surface one(s). This is especially true in the instance of religious texts that are primarily operative in the environment of religious communities that utilize them in ways that are accompanied by their own cultic life and paraphernalia. The fine line at this point between exegesis and eisegesis is a risky one to maintain, but the failure to consider this aspect of the text is to live perpetually in the limited perspectives of the mechanistic view that informs our general culture.

• Primeval Mythos: Yahweh and the Fragility of Time •

When we turn to Genesis 1–11 with these considerations in mind, it becomes clear that the basic Hebrew perspective of creation that is signified in this material is generally presupposed throughout the remainder of the Bible. The implication of this is that creation becomes visible to us as a major component of Old Testament literature, by virtue of its continuing silent vitality throughout the centuries of its formation, reformulation, and repeated reading. As a general rule, in order for a subject to assume textuality, a conflict or dissatisfaction of some sort generally stands behind it. The conflict with the religions of the ancient Near East certainly enabled the Old Testament creation account(s) to achieve textuality, not, for example, the scientific curiosity and/or technological utility that generates contemporary cosmological accounts. These texts are commonly and correctly interpreted in this fashion, based largely on the reiteration of the formulaic "and he [God] said" (וַיֹּאמֶר) in Genesis 1. Acceptance of Yahweh God as the creator of the cosmos was not a contested feature of Yahwism once the issue had been solved in relation to surrounding deities. Therefore, Old Testament texts are relatively silent about this issue throughout the period of their composition. The perspective of Yahweh as creator existed passively as a given theological resource and could be drawn upon at any time by subsequent writers for their own purposes (for example, Exodus 15, Psalm 29, Job 38ff., and the like). In this case, the very silence of the creation tradition in Yahwism was a sign of its strength due to its incontestability. Properly understood, therefore, the Yahwistic creation tradition is one of the strongest ones in the Bible, and it should in no wise be considered secondary to "historical Yahwism." The melting of these two aspects of Yahwism that takes place with the Call of Abraham (Genesis 12:1) stands as a corrective to the limitations of our own linear way of viewing time.

In a recent study relating theology and technology, Egbert Schuurman makes the following statement concerning the theological perspective of Genesis 1–11.

> Since the fall, history has ceased to be the unfolding of creation through the fulfillment of man's cultural task. On the contrary, history has been running ever more aground. Of this the flood, the building of a Babel culture, and the biblical history of Israel are clear manifestations. Nor can man himself restore history. Rather, he is the cause of its many dislocations and destructions. Skills and techniques of all kinds may be admirable, but the tyrannical or greedy use of human power over nature is a failure deriving from human sin, not from God's intention in the creation.

He concludes, "Sin always involves a loss of 'earth' in some sense: alienation from God and alienation from creation go hand in hand."[5] This interpretation of the Old Testament materials has many of the traditional elements of Christian exegesis, and I have chosen to highlight it partly for reasons of contrast with my own reading under the discipline of a critical reading of American ethos. Nonetheless, it correctly points to the underlying structural unity of creation and history that I have emphasized above, albeit a structural unity fractured by the traditional understanding of the Fall. In this view, the Fall severs history from creation in a primordial disruption that can only be reinstituted by God with the Call of Abraham in Genesis 12:1. In this way, while the concerns of the faith are grounded in the traditional Christian idea of the history of salvation, the goal of this salvation history is the restoration of all history and creation.

I would like to make another proposal on the interpretation of Genesis 1–11 that shares several of the features of Schuurman's reading, but one that also differs from it significantly. In particular, I find his proposal that sin always involves a loss of " 'earth' in some sense" to be penetrating and insightful, but one that can also be refined based on our earlier analysis of American texts. Our American texts have repeatedly indicated that, for us, sin is the ability to manipulate time, or, more specifically, to put time in the service of the protection of our place (meaning geographical space). I believe that this perspective is already anticipated in the Primordial History. That is why Genesis 3–11 comes after Genesis 1–2. Genesis 3–11 is the aborted attempt of humans aggressively to manipulate time (i.e., history) for their own self-interests, beginning with the so-called Fall of Genesis 3; an attempt that culminates in the story of the

---

[5]Egbert Schuurman, "A Christian Philosophical Perspective on Technology," in Carl Mitcham and Jim Grote, eds., *Theology and Technology* (Lanham MD, New York, London: University Press of America, 1984) 107–19.

Tower of Babel in Genesis 11. Importantly, the response of Yahweh to each of these outbreaks of human sin is not punishment in a legalistic sense, but consists of acts designed to further protect the fragile created order of the natural interrelation of space and time. This is in stark contrast to the punishment meted out by Noah to the sin of Ham in Genesis 9:25, which is retaliatory in character: "Accursed be Canaan. He shall be his brothers' meanest slave." God acts out of the protection of the created order; humans act out of vengeance. Schuurman is correct in his explanation of why alienation from earth and history (time) go hand in hand. This explains why, according to the Genesis account, human efforts to coalesce human technique with our natural propensity for meaningful work is just as problematic as the fusion of human history and the discernment of God's activity in the world. I might add that this explains why we cannot force the appearance of the Kingdom of God into our space. To *force*, in the sense of the post-Genesis 11 environment, would mean to capture the Kingdom under the terms of our conception of time and space. This would bring about the effect of the "spatializing of time" that has thematized our study of the problematic features of American culture. As we have seen, the spatializing of time carries with it the immediate effect of further alienation. This means that while we have the ability to find security "for a time" in the defense of our space by the manipulation of time (as frequently witnessed in modern technology), this act robs us of the fullness of life itself.

As is well known, several key events take place in Genesis 1–11 that bespeak the emergence of human sin to an extent that calls forth a divine response: the eating of the forbidden fruit, Cain's murder of Abel, the song of Lamech, the marriage of the daughters of men by the sons of God, and the construction of the Tower of Babel. Von Rad believed that this material reflected the perspective of increasing deterioration in the relation between God and humans on the part of the J writer. Furthermore, he saw the increase in human sin as evoking the response of appropriate grace on the part of Yahweh, matching the expressions of human sin, and paving the way for the birth of the Israelite religion denoted in the Call of Abraham. More recently, Old Testament scholars have questioned the idea of the progressive intensification of sin operative in this narrative unit. However, irrespective of this exegetical issue, which is tied to literary-critical concerns, the texts we have studied above in American ethos bring to the front two basic exegetical issues in this material: (1) What is the underlying meaning of the human sin that is perpetrated by humans in the story and (2) is the divine response to be framed in terms of these sinful acts, or in terms of the structure of creation? Specifically, we need to inquire into the theological view of space and time in the narrative that will help us make a better evaluation of the main features of American ethos. Before a more detailed discussion of this problem, it is crucial to point out the central place of Genesis 2:15 in the story: "Yahweh God took the man and settled him in the Garden of Eden *in order to serve and watch it"* (לְעָבְדָהּ וּלְשָׁמְרָהּ)(my translation). This verse now stands in programmatic relationship to the remainder of Genesis 1–11. For the whole of this body of material, therefore, the shape of human work is defined by serving and watching (in the sense of guarding), a perspective that clearly stands in opposition to those features delineated above as major characteristics of the American ethos. Whatever sins are to follow in Genesis 3 and beyond, all of them stem from human rebellion against this posture of serving and watching that the narrative proclaims is intrinsic to the essence of the human condition. As Schuurman correctly indicates, " . . . sin always involves a loss of 'earth' in some sense: alienation from God and alienation from creation go hand in hand." The earth is man's primordial home, and coming from the soil, all other forms of his existence must always come to terms with this fact.

In order to determine the fundamental nature of human sin as it arises in Genesis 1–11, let us observe each occurrence of it in literary context. First, the eating of the forbidden fruit is born out of the human desire to become "as [the] gods" (כֵּאלֹהִים), knowing good and evil (יֹדְעֵי טוֹב וָרָע, Gen. 3:5). The prohibition against eating of this fruit of the tree of the knowledge of good and evil is stipulated in 2:17 and represents the only prohibition given during the time of the actual creation. What is particularly interesting about the story is the rationale for the consequence of banishment from the Garden that ensues upon the completion of the crime. Toward the end of the overall narrative we read, "Yahweh God said: 'Behold, the man has become as one of us, knowing good and evil.' And as a result, lest he stretch out his hand and take (fruit) also from the tree of life, and eat of it, and live forever: Yahweh God sent Adam from the Garden of Eden to serve the soil from which he was taken" (3:22–23). What is particularly instructive about this passage is that Adam's banishment from the Garden takes place as a result of Yahweh's concern for *time,* in the form of the tree of life whose fruit will allow Adam to live *forever.* In other words, Adam is dislocated by Yahweh so that he will not be able to manipulate time in order to fortify his place in the Garden (to "live forever") by eating of the tree of life. Yahweh's punishment of banishment is not effected for the sake of punishment. It is a punishment that arises out of Yahweh's concern for the fragility of time. Whatever else it has accomplished, the human knowledge of good and evil has brought with it the possibility of human manipulation of time. I believe that this text clearly points to this manipulation of time as the primary area where human sin can penetrate with the most damage against the basic structure of creation. In this context, the problems raised by American ethos begin to take on cosmological significance from the biblical perspective. The message of the Bible is clear at this point: the utilization of time for the sake of space results in banishment.

The precise reason why Yahweh rejected the offering from the soil by

Cain in Genesis 4 has been debated by Old Testament interpreters for centuries. It is obvious that the text is not primarily interested in explicitly the reason for Yahweh's negative response. Rather, its focus is on the response itself and Cain's angry reaction to it that results in the murder of his brother out of envy. Because the text is unconcerned with the question of Yahweh's rationale, and rather with Cain's reaction, so will I be. If we penetrate to the deeper levels of the brief narrative, we see the problem of the human control of time as underlying Cain's emotion of envy, but this control of time manifests itself in a different aspect than in Genesis 3 ("living forever"). Here we are dealing with time in an embryonic cause and effect relationship that bridges the present and future. In point of fact, Cain wishes to control the future (Yahweh's response to his offering) based on his act in the present (the presentation of the offering to Yahweh). In this sense, von Rad is correct in pointing to the issue of Yahweh's freedom as being fundamentally at stake in the narrative, even if we believe that certain intimations exist as to the rationale (the ground had been cursed, or the like). The meaning of Yahweh's freedom is that the future is his, and not Cain's. Cain cannot force either Yahweh's future or his own by a rationalistic approach based on cause and effect. Whether Yahweh has sufficient grounds (from a human standpoint) to act in the way in which he does is of no interest to the writer. This glaring omission in the narrative only emphasizes the point of Cain's desire to manipulate the future, yet his inability to do so. The protection of time from human control is thereby maintained in the course of primordial events. Even Cain himself is protected from further consequences of his deed by human hands when Yahweh places the mark upon him. This act continues the theme of the narrative of Yahweh's ongoing intention of the protection of creation, rather than punishment of human sin.

From a literary-critical standpoint, one of the oldest texts in the Old Testament is the song of Lamech (4:23–24). It is generally classified as having originally been an oral boasting or a revenge song, and it is considered to have originated at a time when the law of blood revenge was circumscribed by little or no restraint. In this original setting, the song celebrated the power of the male hero who was able to protect his wives in a hostile environment, devoid of a written law code or a state controlled legal system. In this situation, it is not so much blood vengeance that is at stake, rather it is the honor of the hero. In its adaptation to the written narrative of Genesis 1–11, however, the text underwent a radical transformation. In its new literary environment, it represents another instance of the outbreak of sin in the primordial context in the guise of Lamech's hubris and brutality. It is not blood vengeance as such that characterizes the passage, but the extent of the blood vengeance that reaches far into the future (seventy-seven-fold vengeance). As with the previous passage, we again find a narrative exposition of the human attempt to manipulate the future, only now set completely within the human context. However, the text does not actually narrate the occurrence of this vengeance, simply the boasting of it in the present to the wives Adah and Zillah. It is this reaching into the future by Lamech, and the celebration of his ability to capture and conquer future events in the present, that gives the text its distinctive characteristic with regard to time. Thus, although the tree of life remains protected from man in the Garden, and Yahweh's own independence has been established through the Cain and Abel story, Lamech now nurtures the human aspiration for the control of time solely within the human realm. The path toward the destruction of the Flood is now firmly established.

The Flood itself is directly motivated in the primordial narrative by the mating of the sons of God and the daughters of men (6:1–4). The implication is clear in this terse account that a major breakdown is indicated by these events that fracture the proper relationship between the divine and human realms. The immediate result of the transposition of the divine beings into creation is a further circumscription of human time: "His days shall be not more than 120 years." By implication, the great danger of the mating of godly and human figures is the creation of beings who could mount yet another attack upon time by approaching the immortality of their divine fathers. Yahweh's response is necessarily severe and specifically addresses the problem of time. Only by limiting the length of human days can the fragility of time be protected and its integrity maintained. The attack upon time is indicated in the passage with the reference to the Nephilim and the designation "men/warriors of eternity" (הַגִּבֹּרִים אֲשֶׁר מֵעוֹלָם [6:4]). Again, as in earlier instances of human sin, Yahweh's response is not conceptualized in the mode of punishment, but in that of the protector of time in the created order.

The story of the construction of the Tower of Babel in Genesis 11 brings the human attack on time to a resounding climax in the Primordial History. While the top of the tower reaches the heavens (וְרֹאשׁוֹ בַשָּׁמַיִם), thereby symbolizing the human attempt to breach the created order, the fundamental rationale for its construction lies in its durability rather than its height. The purpose of the construction is clearly manifested in the statement that men wanted to "make a name for themselves" (וְנַעֲשֶׂה־לָּנוּ שֵׁם).[6] This is also the reason why the materials of the construction are explicitly stated in far greater detail than would otherwise be expected. These are materials that are noted for their lasting qualities: " 'Come, let us make bricks and bake them in the fire.' For stone they used bricks, and for mortar they used bitumen" (11:3). The tone of this story is as tragic as

---

[6]Robert A. Oden, Jr., "Divine Aspirations in Atrahasis and in Genesis 1–11," *Zeitschrift für die alttestamentliche Wissenschaft* 93:2 (1981): 214, writes, "That they (the first humans) should immediately attempt to establish for themselves a lasting reputation, as did the masons in Gen. 11, is predictable. . . ."

it is loathsome. Having failed in all other ways to deny the natural place of time in the natural order, the building of the tower is the final human attempt in the Primordial History to manipulate time by capturing the future and bringing it under human control. The tower is the symbolic embodiment of the spatializing of time for all future generations. It is the enduring biblical symbol of technology carried to a purely rationalistic extreme. The divine response of confusing human tongues and scattering them over all the face of the earth is again meant to thwart the human attack on time, and not as a punishment. This is the final divine act before the new language of religion is issued in Genesis 12 with the call of Abraham by Yahweh.

• Gnostic Mythos: Yahweh and the Delusion of Time •

The ancient Gnostic movement had its origins several centuries after the final composition of the Primordial History and was as greatly influenced by it as was Christian orthodoxy. It represents a major option in the way the Primeval History could be read from an antagonistic theological perspective. It is instructive for our hermeneutical interests to consider briefly this Gnostic reading as a mirror that reflects the extremes such a reading may take, and as a guide for explicating the antagonist features present in our own cultural reading. Like the original humans imaginatively portrayed in Genesis 1–11, Gnosticism aimed to destroy the fabric of creation at its most vulnerable interpretive point: time. The Gnostic fallacy, correctly identified by orthodoxy, was its necessary attack upon the religion of Yahweh and its stance against the control and manipulation of time. On the other hand, the religion of Jesus, bereft of this Yahwistic element, was not opposed by the Gnostics, rather it was adopted and adapted to this antagonistic theology. This Gnosticizing tendency tempts us in every age, especially so in the age of industrialized technology. The Orthodox Christian rejection of the Gnostic reading remains paradigmatic for every generation of Christians, and it has special relevance to American biblical hermeneutics because of the centrality of this problem of time in its thought.

At the heart of problematic Gnostic existence was the question of the character of creation. In the face of the ultimate mysteries of human existence, it posited an alien and hostile world. Because the god of the Old Testament was acknowledged as creator of this world, he was judged to be an inferior and ignorant deity: inferior because the product he created was a counterfeit image of the truly divine, ignorant because he did not recognize this fact. This utilization of the Judaic creation tradition by the Gnostics illustrates a blatantly polemical perspective operative in their theology,[7] one we might characterize in terms of negative dialectics rather

---

[7]See Hans Jonas, "The Gnostic Syndrome: Typology of Its Thought, Imagination, and Mood," in *Philosophical Essays: From Ancient Creed to Technological Man,* ed. Hans Jonas (Chicago: University of Chicago Press, 1974) 263–76, esp. 273–74.

than hermeneutics in the traditional sense. We know that Christianity grew up in the midst of Judaic apocalyptic traditions. Without these currents of thought shaping and nurturing the development of the church, subsequent Christian development would not be recognizable to us. But Christian orthodoxy decided to redirect Jewish apocalypticism rather than discredit it—a decision that had enormous consequences for the subsequent development of Western science and technology.

More than a generation ago, Henri-Charles Peuch identified correctly the heart of Gnostic world-anxiety in the traditional philosophical problem of permanence and change, that is, time.[8] We may take the (Valentinian) Gospel of Philip as characteristic of this Gnostic worldview: "The world came about through a mistake. For he who created it wanted to create it imperishable and immortal. He fell short of attaining his desire. For the world never was imperishable, nor, for that matter, was he who made the world" (Gospel of Philip 75.2–9).[9] Here we see that the world is considered to have come about as a result of a cosmic mistake. This mistakenness of the world is evident to all in its perishability and mortality. Generally, this way of interpreting nature is commonly termed devolution in the scholarly literature, that is, a movement into the lower regions of the cosmos, which are ruled by time.

The Gnostic treatise entitled "On the Origin of the World" (97.24–98.7) begins its probe of the status of this chaotic impermanence of the world in this way:

> Since everyone—the gods of the world and men—says that nothing has existed prior to Chaos, I shall demonstrate that [they] all erred, since they do not know the [structure] of Chaos and its root. Here [is the] demonstration:
> If it is [agreed by] all men concerning [Chaos] that it is a darkness, then it is something derived from a shadow. It was called darkness.
> But the shadow is something derived from a work existing from the beginning.
> So it is obvious that it [the first work] existed before Chaos came into being, which followed after the first work.

This text points to an immutable reality that exists before the present chaotic reality ruled by time. The document goes on to explain the origin of this "shadow" as arising from the outward part of the region of immeasurable light (truth). It is viewed as the root of all evil in the world. From it sprang the race of the gods of this world, including the God of the Old

---

[8]Henri-Charles Puech, "Gnosis and Time," in *Man and Time*, ed. Joseph Campbell, Bollingen Series 30 (Princeton: Princeton University Press, 1983) 38–84.

[9]All textual references from Gnostic texts are taken from James M. Robinson, ed., *The Nag Hammadi Library in English* (San Francisco: Harper & Row, 1977).

Testament, often named Jaldabaoth, "begetter of the (heavenly) powers."[10] The intention of the Gnostic movement was to bring about salvation from this world and its gods through the saving knowledge of the ineffable "unknown" God who exists in the timeless *Pleroma* (the "fullness" beyond the cosmos). However, "On the Origin of the World" (99.2–22) points to something even more primary than the gods when it discusses the origin of matter. We find this description of reality before the birth of the gods:

> Then the shadow perceived that there was one stronger than it. It was jealous, and when it became self-impregnated, it immediately bore envy. Since that day the origin of envy has appeared in all of the aeons and their worlds. But that envy was found to be a miscarriage without any spirit in it. It became like the shadows in a great watery substance. Then the bitter wrath which came into being from the shadow was cast into a region of Chaos. . . . Just as all the useless afterbirth of one who bears a little child falls, likewise the matter which came into being from the shadow was cast aside. And it did not come out of Chaos, but matter was in Chaos, (existing) in a part of it.

We learn here that the origin of matter was bound up with the interplay of primeval light and shadow, particularly the affection of envy, which welled up in the latter upon perceiving the former. The introduction of envy at this primeval state explains the destructive character that time perpetrates on matter. Eventually, in this mythology, the god Jaldabaoth is born at the bidding of the immortal feminine principle named Pistis Sophia ("Faith/Wisdom") out of the watery chaos in order to rule over matter and its powers. This god creates out of matter both his own dwelling place ("heaven") and the earth. In the Gnostic mind, salvation consists of escaping the clutches of both the envious god and the "envious" character of matter that holds the eternally divine "spark" or "spirit" of man in captivity, alienated from its true home in the divine, eternal world. In this way, the entire worldview of Judaism and Christian orthodoxy is undermined and discredited.

• Biblical Technique versus Modern Technique •

*In an effort to hinder the biblical reader from manipulating and controlling time in the interpretation of biblical texts, redactors of the biblical canon developed their own forms of dialogical technique that allowed for

---

[10]Kurt Rudolph, *Gnosis: The Nature and History of Gnosticism*, trans. Robert McLachlan Wilson (San Francisco: Harper & Row, 1983) 73.

*Pages 97–104 appeared in a similar form in an article entitled "Biblical Hermeneutics and the Critique of Technology," in Carl Mitcham and Jim Grote, eds., *Theology and Technology* (Lanham, New York, London: University Press of America, 1984) 157–69.

the play of time even as it protected it. As a result, what we might term "biblical technique" tends to be far less aggressive than modern managerial technique in that it assumes its final shape within a dialogical, open-ended structure. The framers of the Christian Bible successfully resist the easy solution of imposing universal theological structures from an autonomous rational standpoint. Much of the current discussion in narrative criticism and reader-response criticism has been helpful in elucidating this phenomenon, and it need not be repeated here. I will only highlight three specific ways that this passive, organic technique is in evidence: (1) the "New" Testament, (2) the quadric nature of the gospel witness, and (3) biblical pluralism.

A major way the Bible exhibits its nonmechanical hermeneutics of time is seen in the relation of the "New" (Greek) and "Old" (Hebrew) Testaments. In general, Jesus is legitimized by prooftexting. The use of these traditions is dictated primarily by the exigencies of the early church, with appropriate techniques employed by which they might be included in the composition of the Hellenistic document. Above all else, one finds massive utilization of typological exegesis with regard to this issue. However, it is of paramount importance to take into account adequately the phenomenon that the Christian canon allows the Old Testament to stand on its own, without interpretation, before it offers an interpretation of selected parts of it. What other major religion is as tolerant of the writings of another religion? Thus, a dialogical structure is established whereby the identity of the already present text is established as a preliminary step in the dialogical process itself. Only in this way is dialogue possible. However, a fundamental ambiguity remains for Christian theology in the way that the New Testament relates to the Old. In fact, Christian theology has failed until our very day to resolve this ambiguity. The canonical framers indicate to us that the Old Testament is at once accepted independently within the context of its own oneness, even as it is interpreted and commented upon by the New. In this way, for the Christian Bible, the Old Testament is simultaneously the story of God with his people and the story of God's preparation for the advent of Jesus Christ.

To amplify this point: the early church initially allowed the Hebrew Scriptures their full and independent voice (albeit in the guise of "the old") in the theology of the canon. This voice often existed silently alongside those enhanced parts of these texts deemed of particular importance from the new Christian standpoint. The latter became a part of the New Testament; the former did not. However, while certain Hebrew perspectives are enhanced in the New Testament and brought into new textual context, the Old Testament is never displaced, and its holistic integrity is never compromised. Upon this dialogical technique of textual interpretation, the basic dialectical structure of Christian existence was established. Therefore, while Christian theology would strive for universality, it would be a universality that would only take shape in dialogue with other religions and cultures. Christianity would be firmly established at its core as a dialectical religion. In fact, the very first verse of the New Testament would establish the entire textual corpus: "A genealogy of Jesus Christ, son of David, son of Abraham" (Matthew 1:1). In one sense, the Hebrew David was of importance to Christians only because, through the eyes of faith, Jesus Christ was to be his "son". But, on the other hand, the story of King David had intrinsic worth for the Christian, as well, and was included in its entirety within the canon. This dialectical perspective strongly resists reduction to systematization. It is a technique that forces the written word to extend its boundaries beyond the limitations that normally constrain it. The "New" Testament would only be new in a complementary sense, not in an aggressive or manipulative sense. The spirit of metaphysics at this point is diametrically opposed to that of modern technique.

In addition, we may well note that the approach of the canonical framers of the Christian Bible to include within it the entire "Old" Testament means that hermeneutics was established not simply as a matter of adjustment and refinement for Christian theology, but as a theological imperative. This imperative is born in the view that naturally unfolds out of the logic of the biblical structure, namely, that the written word remain flexible enough to be continually challenged and confronted anew by the march of history and the change of perspective thereby implied. Within the believing community, this is meant to insure that the written word not become an obstacle to the final goal of living faith, but an aid to it. But the same vitality remains for a more general public reading of the Scriptures as well. Both early Christianity and Pharisaic Judaism took this dialogical approach to the Old Testament tradition, but Christianity alone assumed such a radical dialogical posture by creating new canonical texts. The more aggressive, monological postures exhibited in other theological movements of the first several centuries failed to survive this dynamic challenge of orthodoxy.

The fact that the church opted against the more rationally efficient way of dealing with the living Judaic tradition by simply eliminating the Old Testament from the Christian Bible (as Marcion and others advocated) confirmed that the hermeneutics of dialogue would dominate a radically monistic technique that would have done away with an independent Jewish voice in Christian thought once and for all. Thus, Christian hermeneutics would be established as dialogical hermeneutics, an approach that listens to the voice of the other before it interprets, regulates, and gives meaning. This is an open hermeneutics that allows the other to be *more than*[11] what one first of all makes use of hermeneutically. As such, the surplus of material in the Old Testament (those passages that had little or no reference to Jesus Christ or Christian life) would remain as new data for

---

[11]Note Paul Ricoeur's notion of "surplus meaning" intrinsic to a text.

later ages to engage and discuss. Furthermore, this whole way of conceiving faith would be paradigmatic for a public reading of the Bible, in that it requires the independent voice of the other for its completion. Thus, while many areas of life addressed in the Old Testament are left in silence in the New, they still retain their vitality for Christian thought. Only in a falsely literalistic sense do we not consider issues as high priority aspects for Christian life and thought. The New Testament hermeneutical interest in the Old Testament as substantiating Jesus as Yahweh's universal offer of salvation ought to be taken as a model for all Christian approaches to it, not as an all-inclusive word. In this way, the breadth of Old Testament religious reflection retains its priority for Christian thought.

The dialogical technique of the Bible that protects the fragility of time from analytical systematization is maintained in a second way by the structure of the New Testament witness to the narrative of the life of Jesus. This arises from the evident, yet striking, fact that it contains four gospels rather than one. The quadric manifestation of the gospels must be interpreted theologically, not simply historically. It is insufficient to note that each gospel sheds additional light upon the historical Jesus, even though this is the case. Such analysis lies in the domain of the techniques of historical criticism. But the fact of four, authorized accounts of Jesus indicates an important theological perspective as well. Rather than a hierarchy of gospels to be read in a certain chronological sequence, the four gospels have the quality of simultaneity. Any one of them can be read first, last, or in between. No proper reading order exists; not one of them presupposes or requires the reading of another. In addition, the implication of this pluralistic gospel witness is that the interpreters of the life of Jesus assume the stature of essential and indivisible importance alongside the historical personage of Jesus himself.[12]

Written words are more one-dimensional in their meaning than oral ones. Also, the tendency of a written account of someone's life is to be either biographical or to be heavily imbued with the particular viewpoint of the author. The fourfold character of the gospels shifts the locus of the account of Jesus toward the audience. Variation in the ways that Jesus is perceived is not only permitted but encouraged. While the movement of journalistic biography tends to be from the many readers to the one (correct) account of a person's life, the movement of the gospels is from the one life of Jesus to the pluralistic audient communities. This movement is not be confused with fiction (as in a fable or fairy tale). For us, however,

---

[12]Robert S. Corrington notes Royce's position on this issue as follows: "Without the hermeneutic manipulations of the community the tradition could not have survived in the long run. Hence Royce seats the locus of Christianity in the hermeneutic acts of the primitive church" (Robert S. Corrington, *The Community of Interpreters* [Macon GA: Mercer University Press, 1987] 72).

it serves as a brake upon the objectivizing tendency present in the modern historicized approach to biographical writing. It is not convincing to argue that the framers of the Bible did not see the chronological problems present when the gospels were compared, for example, the chronology connected with Jesus' visit to Jerusalem. Yet, the early church chose to live within this tension, rather than sacrifice the dialogical technique of relating his life to the various audiences that were addressed and bend in the direction of a systematized account that portrays the one "correct" chronological sequence of events. In this way, the plurality of approaches to the life of Jesus represents a technique that enhances the basic properties inherent in narrative that invite comparison and a further unfolding of the meaning of his life within the various communities that place themselves within historic Christianity.

The decision to canonize the community's remembrances of Jesus in this pluralistic fashion highlights the place of subjectivism and individuality in the biblical tradition. And, it is at this point that a major tension exists between the dialogical technique characteristic of the Bible and the worldview of modern technology. The gospels are born and nurtured in the context of living faith and thus resist any attempt to transpose them into simplistically objective accounts of the life of Jesus. Luke, the most historical of the gospels in terms of expressed intentionality, did not achieve the same degree of popularity in the early church as did Matthew. The interplay of a gospel with the subjective particularities of community experience is of higher value than its objective historical reliability. The subjective orientation of the gospels in their multifarious unfolding of Jesus' life and its meaning implies a certain incompleteness that stimulates the active involvement of the biblical reader in the interpretive task in a way unknown to the modern historian who judges by the standards of objectivity.

This subjectivity does not displace the historicity of the story of Jesus, rather it tempers it with the historicity of the audience. If just any subjective interpretation of Jesus had been accepted as encouraged by the canonical gospels, then, as we know from recent Gnostic discoveries, the realm of the antihistorical would have been included in the canon. Today, we see more clearly than before that the gospels do exhibit a common field of understanding and agreement with regard to theological perspective, in spite of the breadth of approaches that is tolerated. If the gospels reflected a random approach to the process of canonization with no obvious theological considerations illustrated, then the designation of "technique" would hardly be appropriate. However, the pluralistic perspectives rooted within a fundamental theological program promote a dialogue between the life of Jesus and the life of the reader, which is anchored in the textual dialogue between the written gospels themselves. This is a passive, listening technique that fractures the constrictions of the written word by refusing to determine in advance what the final configuration of Christian belief will be. It is a technique that is alive, less subject to the natural alienation of (written) language that conceals as well as reveals, because it promotes the growth and development of a Jesus who transcends our humanly imposed chronological perspectives.

Finally, the entire range of biblical pluralism acts as a safeguard against the tendency of interpretive reductionism, always a temptation in ecclesiastically dominated Christian theology with its impetus toward the authoritative account of God's *historical* presence with his people. By way of background, let us recall that a categorical shift takes place when the spoken word is transformed into the written word. Speaking is the miraculous gift of nature to man; writing, on the other hand, is the miraculous invention of man. We think of speaking as natural and writing as technical. There is a living quality present in the spoken word that is absent in the written word, making speaking the more dependent on the other (audience) and, hence, the more dialogical of the two.[13] Normally, outside the modern electronic technologies, which give speech a written character, speaking is done within a particular, well-defined community. The essence of genuine dialogue lies in the fact that "each of the participants really has in mind the other or others in their present and particular being and turns to them with the intention of establishing a living mutual relation between himself and them."[14] A major problem for any writer is the inability to see "the other," that is, the audience. This one-dimensional, and frequently oppressive, tendency of the written word is especially operative in such community or public documents as religious scriptures. It follows, as well, that from a theological point of view, the modern technological age represents an especially profound threat to the

---

[13]Perhaps the best introduction to the pioneering work done by Walter J. Ong, S.J., in this field is his little handbook *Orality and Literacy: The Technologizing of the Word* (London and New York: Methuen, 1982). Ong writes, "The condition of words in a text is quite different from their condition in spoken discourse. Although they refer to sounds and are meaningless unless they can be related— externally or in the imagination—to the sounds or, more precisely, the phonemes they encode, written words are isolated from the fuller context in which spoken words come into being. The word in its natural, oral habitat is a part of a real, existential present. Spoken utterance is addressed by a real, living person to another real, living person or real, living persons, at a specific time in a real setting which includes always much more than mere words. Spoken words are always modifications of a total situation which is more than verbal. They never occur alone, in a context simply of words.

Yet words are alone in a text. Moreover, in composing a text, in 'writing' something, the one producing the written utterance is also alone. *Writing is a solipsistic operation*" [my emphasis] (p. 101).

[14]This definition comes from Maurice Friedman, *Martin Buber: The Life of Dialogue*, 3rd ed. (Chicago: University of Chicago Press, 1976) 87.

spoken character of the Bible by allowing the frequently uncritical philosophical presuppositions of the technological worldview to dominate in the interpretation of the text. The result is a still further drain upon the life of the biblical word, beyond that dispersed through the transition in most of its texts from spoken to written language. In a very subtle fashion, the entire character of the Bible itself is shifted into a new key, one that tends to affirm and substantiate the technological age rather than remain outside of it.

Biblical pluralism, therefore, rejects any interpretation that makes the Bible itself the supreme object of religious faith, or, better, any particular way of reading the Bible. This pluralism is found within the Old Testament, the New Testament, and the relationship between the two cultures that generated them. It has the effect of helping maintain the spoken, dialogical quality of the written text. Thus, the intrinsic dominance of the written word over its audience is mollified in the Bible by its own internal dialogical form. This is true in terms of divergent content, multiple literary sources and genres, and distinct languages and cultural perspectives. The promonarchical and antimonarchical voices in the Old Testament maintain their identities, just as the various titles of Jesus remain unsystematized in the New Testament. The divergent theologies of the Yahwistic and Priestly sources of the Pentateuch make their contributions to the biblical message, just as do those of Mark and the Q source. When the New Testament proclaims Jesus in Greek terms as the *christ*, a whole new field of meaning is introduced into the tradition that exceeds the boundaries of the Hebrew term *messiah*.

This technical pluralism acts as a brake toward the aggressive, monistic qualities of the modern technological worldview. In fact, modern attempts to synthesize technologically the entire message of the Bible into a constitution of religious beliefs represents a crucial insight into modernity. The Bible simply rejects an all-inclusive, systematic synthesis of its views and perspectives. The modern attempt to systematize, to the degree that it dominates theological understanding, is a betrayal of the dialogical spirit the Bible demands of its readers. The fabric of the Bible itself, with its techniques of repetition, disjunctive narrative chronology, fictional and factual blending, and the like, is simply not congruent with the foundational worldview of modern technology. In the Bible, diversity is held in as high esteem as unity, because whatever unity exists, exists in the divine sphere rather than the human or natural. This dependency upon the object of faith transcends the autonomous claims that any particular tradition, social class, or theological perspective might make if left unchecked by the plurality of streams flowing into its construction. This plurality results in a kind of vagueness that many in our time see simply as an object to be overcome in the technologization of the Bible in the modern vein, rather than a phenomenon to be interpreted by theology. The diversity of opinion, which allows, for example, the books of Job and

Ecclesiastes to arise out of the older, exhausted intellectual traditions of the wise, is a lesson in the technique of dialogue that transpires within biblical texts. The spectrum of theological diversity in the Old Testament was broad enough to stretch from Deuteronomy and Proverbs to Job and Ecclesiastes. This dialogue within the written word sets the mode that the reader must assume in order to begin the process of interpretation. It is an invitational mode that beckons us to join in a *common* venture of faith by allying our voice to the voices of the past. The plurality of written voices and traditions results in a kind of transparency that forces us to focus our attention on the faith of the Bible that has generated its technique, but is never identical with it. It is written technique that stands partially transformed into the living force of the spoken word for which it yearns.

• Conclusion •

In our day, one finds a growing dissatisfaction with the direction of the modern technological world among many adherents to the Christian tradition. Others, more impressed with the achievements of technology, speak of our time as "the post-Christian era," a designation that not so much disavows the truth claims of Christianity as it finds them irrelevant. In either case, the challenge of the new technology to the historical Christian faith with its foundations in the Bible is formidable. Our discussion of technology above, set in the context of American democratic consciousness, has revealed that the utilization and control of time is the interior reality of technology. The questions of ultimate concern, which Tillich and others have so thoughtfully expounded to us, have themselves become secondary to the management of time for an increasing number of people. Thus, from a theological perspective, the real achievement of modern technology is to make the penultimate questions (means), ultimate (ends) and to make traditionally ultimate questions, penultimate. This is the threat upon their tradition that many believers sense intuitively, but they find the relevant theological categories so very difficult to articulate.

The evidence is strong that the achievement of modern technology points to a shift in history as profound as any previous axial age (noted by Karl Jaspers and others). If the prophecies of Jacques Ellul, and those who join him in the denunciations of modern technology, are even suggestive of the truth, then Christian theology is faced with a monumental task. Something new has entered the world and nothing explicit in the biblical tradition is equal to the challenge that this poses. The heart of Christian tradition show a desire to reach out to all of humanity from a posture of dialogue. Such a stance toward the varieties of human experience is foreign to the aggressive character of the modern technological world. According to the biblical claim, God is very slow and *inefficient* in his dealings with the human race. The speed and efficiency valued so highly in contemporary times stands in stark contrast to this view.

The ancient Gnostics correctly perceived that a certain view of time lay at the topological center of Jewish and Christian orthodoxy. The interior struggle over exterior theological issues, for example, Christology, the place of the Law, and the like, dealt with this issue at the deepest theological levels. The Gnostics' effective elimination of time as a theological category, rather than its utilization, was rightly rejected by Christian orthodoxy. Had their concept of the absolute alienation of humanity from time (and, hence, creation itself) generally persuaded the church, then the view of matter and time presupposed by scientific empiricism and technical efficiency ironically could not have emerged. The decision of orthodoxy to develop a chronologically centered hermeneutics enabled it to claim for its own what it considered the heart of Jewish tradition, including the foundation of a positive view of nature. It would remain for later generations to work out the implications of maintaining the entire Old Testament in full partnership with the New Testament canon. American biblical hermeneutics indicates that the fundamental theological problem still to be resolved is the meaning of the chronological designations *old* and *new* testaments. The contemporary technological worldview that dominates in America, with its inherent manipulation of time, has pushed this issue to the top of the theological agenda. The Gnostic tributary within the early church helps clarify the depth of the problem of time for the faith, and it is of fundamental importance in developing our own hermeneutical strategies.

The above study reveals a basic flaw in the modern study of the Bible. This flaw is tied to two perceptions of the problem of context in interpretation, and may be delineated as follows: the prior context for reading biblical material is not the external ancient Near East (Old Testament) nor the Hellenistic world (New Testament), but its own interior cultural preunderstanding. Technology tends to direct us toward outward and external realities, modern archaeology being but one of numerous examples. Our infatuation with the external enables us to bypass the far more complex and elusive interior world of the text. Although descriptions of the historical contexts that nurtured the formation of the Bible given to us by the historical-critical methodologies play important secondary roles in more refined explanations of the Bible, they ought not displace the silent meanings accompanying these texts that are grounded in cultural presuppositions. These presuppositions continue to have their effect through succeeding generations of interpretation.

These observations suggest that a "theology of community" (ancient Israel/primitive church) should precede the traditional one of biblical (or Old/New Testament) theology. In a recent important article, Old Testament theologian Rolf Knierim makes this observation in a passing footnote: "One may question whether an appropriate understanding of Israel's concept of history is possible without a sufficient understanding of Israel's concept of reality. That such an understanding must be reconstructed from our texts is obvious since nowhere has the Old Testament given us a systematic treatise of this subject."[15] The interpretation I have given above of Genesis 1–11 is an attempt at a reconstruction of the ancient Israelite concept of reality that stands behind much of the Old Testament. It should be recalled that the ancient Israelite religion was not a "religion of the book" in the sense of modern fundamentalism. The texts of this culture were constructed upon previously existing structures of thought. A major task within the scope of biblical hermeneutics is the uncovering of those structures of thought in ancient Israel and the early church, and engaging them from the critical context of our own interior constructions of reality. We might put the matter in this way: The Old Testament represents the way ancient Israel related itself to a particular view of the world that existed for the most part silently alongside those texts that it generated. We need to recognize that our own tendency to think in terms of the full meaning of the text being explicitly present in its words stems from our worldview, and not that of the texts themselves. In Old Testament cosmological texts, for example, indications of a much more comprehensive view of reality become at least partly visible, as we have seen.

The consequence of these observations is a different understanding of the character of biblical texts than is commonly held. Frequently, the presupposed worldview is intimated rather than being directly signified. It is important to remember, as well, that the intention of the Old Testament is not to clarify the way ancient Israel understood reality, but to relate its historical experience to the received view. Genesis 1–11 (in addition to other isolated cosmological texts) is an indication that the religious faith of ancient Israel was grounded in an interior theology of world. This point of view laid a foundation for the understanding of its historical experience, but it represented a theological tradition that never explicitly assumed its rightful place in Israel's textual tradition because it ultimately was less problematical than the historical component of Israel's religious experience. This interpretation must necessarily be a reconstructed one in part, because it runs silently alongside the expressed textual purposes found throughout both the Old and New Testaments. Furthermore, the difficulties inherent in such scholarly reconstructions indicate a certain hiddenness in the biblical text, which I believe must itself be taken up into the interpretive process. In particular, if we agree that interior theologies of ancient Israel exist alongside exterior textual theologies of the Old Testament, then it is not in the text that we must ultimately confront them, but in the world of our own experience. In this sense, the silent meaning of the text forces us back upon our own experience as the place where we ultimately encounter the faith that generated these very same texts.

---

[15]Rolf Knierim, "Cosmos and History in Israel's Theology," *Horizons in Biblical Theology* (1982): 115.

SubTEXT: Time and American Theology

The Ramist reworking of dialectic and rhetoric furthered the elimination of sound and voice from man's understanding of the intellectual world and helped create within the human spirit itself the silences of a spatialized universe.[1]

• Theology in the American Locus •

Until now, attempts to think about the American religious experience have been conceived on a spatial model: American theology bound to the geographical locus of the United States and the people who live within it. American theology is presumed to have an independent objective reality that is "out there" to be discovered by the careful scholar. It is this objectivity, or *thingness*, that the dialectics of American biblical hermeneutics has the potential to overcome. The ontological insight of Harold Oliver is central here.

> Physical time and space are derived from features of experience, but—as they function in modern physics—represent no more than the language of measurement. In modern physics, informed by quantum and relativity theory, "things" are no longer said to be "located" in space and time. Even the usual notion of "thing" has been replaced by that of space-time events. Nevertheless there remain philosophers and theologians who continue to use this questionable idiom in the fundamental way in which these notions functioned in Newtonian Physics. The result is often "a misplaced concreteness" applied to time and space.[2]

Following Oliver and others, it is more insightful to think in terms of

---

[1]Walter J. Ong, S.J., *Ramus, Method, and the Decay of Dialogue* (Cambridge MA: Harvard University Press, 1983) 318.

[2]Harold H. Oliver, *Relatedness: Essays in Metaphysics and Theology* (Macon GA: Mercer University Press, 1984) 70.

"space-time" events, than of "things" located in space and time.[3] Applying these insights of modern physics to the worldview in which we read the Bible today, we see that it is reductionistic to interpret America as the concrete locus in which we are to investigate our religious heritage. Our study of the modern technological mind has exhibited to us the centrality of spatialized time in modern thought.[4]

In an authentic sense, America is not a place, it is an event of imaginative possibility. This fact was first seen by the early Puritan framers of the New England experience, and it eventually became a view generalized throughout the land. I take the work of Sacvan Bercovitch as propaedeutic. He writes, "The Puritans provided the scriptural basis for what we have come to call the myth of America."[5] He goes on to show that the sanctification of Puritan society was accomplished hermeneutically by "discovering America in the Bible," a process of sanctification that subsequently became the basis for the fully developed American myth that was eventually extended throughout the culture.[6] I would term this process nothing less than a refashioning of the Bible into a public text for the American experience that both included and exceeded its ecclesiastical origins. Puritan religion, and eventually the mainstream of the American religion generally, replaced the traditional rituals of the church with the "ritual of the word."[7] A public hermeneutics of the Bible in the American setting has its intellectual origins in this Puritan exegetical methodology. Therefore, America, unique in world history, was established on the basis of the power of *words*, on a particular interpretation of history—and

---

[3]This is in line with Whitehead, who believes that we never perceive things, but only events. Cf. Bertrand P. Helm, *Time and Reality in American Philosophy* (Amherst: University of Massachusetts Press, 1985) 143.

[4]In a recent study, Michael Storper and Richard Walker argue persuasively that capitalism achieves a "place-bound mastery of technology" as it effects a revolution of "the forces and relations of production, the conditions of social life, and the course of human history." See Storper and Walker, *The Capitalist Imperative: Territory, Technology, and Industrial Growth* (New York, Oxford: Basil Blackwell, 1989) 227.

[5]Sacvan Bercovitch, "The Biblical Basis of the American Myth," in *The Bible and American Arts and Letters* (Philadelphia: Fortress; Chico CA: Scholars, 1983) 219. Bercovitch goes on to write, "It is not too much to say that the Puritans replaced the traditional rituals of the church (Anglican as well as Catholic) with the rituals of the word: the texts of scripture, interpreted ad tedium in sermons and treatises, privately applied in diaries, memoirs, and journals, publicly affirmed in histories, almanacs, poems, and biographies, and re-presented day by day in the lives of visible saints" (p. 221).

[6]Ibid., 223.

[7]Ibid., 221.

the Bible would serve as the cornerstone for that interpretation.[8]

The false way of conceiving the task of theology in the American "place" utilizes the power of words as a defense *for* the religious point of view of the American people. Interestingly, in this manner of expression, the original spatial connotation remains. It denotes the process of staking out the particular "ground" from which theological issues may be addressed. (It is not happenstance that in argumentation we speak of "mapping out a position.") Indeed, the idea of place is commonly present in the deeper layers of our language when we think of it as "a situation or state relative to circumstances." In this sense, Western Christian theology is typically place or position oriented, in that it is established within the boundary of Christian understanding, itself existing within the intellectual matrix of the world in which it finds itself.

I believe that this spatial way of conceptualizing our (religious) experience has meant that Western theology has been unduly restricted in its development because this spatial way of thinking has externalized our religious experience. This has been especially true in America because this perspective runs counter to the deeper meaning of the ethos grounded in democracy. My thesis is that we need to recast the way we read the Bible, beginning with the parameters of this ethos, in order to interiorize it for a fuller and richer religious understanding.[9] This process of interiorization can only begin with the recognition of our common mental structure that exteriorizes the Bible. Certainly, the task in accomplishing this is formidable. We must, it seems, *dis*place our own narrowly drawn surface ethos in order to open up the new ground of American biblical hermeneutics and open the possibility of a revivified theology. In a larger sense, I propose that the morphology of our theology itself be *dis*placed (in the sense of *de*place) as well. Striving toward this goal represents the authentically universal ramifications of American biblical hermeneutics, as well as American religious thought in toto.

---

[8]Bercovitch describes the Puritan origins of the American myth as follows: "The Puritans came to America not to usurp but to reclaim, not to displace an alien culture but to repossess what was already theirs by promise. And the promise entailed a full-scale myth, with a beginning, a middle, and an end. On one side was the Bible; on the other, the millennium; and at the center, a saintly remnant on a special mission, for America first and then the world" (p. 223).

[9]Relative to this point, Josiah Royce writes: "My thesis is that, in the present state of the world's civilization, and of the life of our own country, the time has come to emphasize, with a new meaning and intensity, the positive value, the absolute necessity for our own welfare, of a wholesome provincialism, as a saving power to which the world in the near future will need more and more to appeal" (quoted in Robert S. Corrington, *The Community of Interpreters: On the Hermeneutics of Nature and the Bible in the American Philosophical Tradition* [Macon GA: Mercer University Press, 1988] 74).

But a theology displaced in favor of what? The texts that we have examined above indicate clearly that the category of time is especially problematical in both our cultural ethos and in biblical texts. If we determine that our way of thinking is unduly spatial, then we are drawn to consider the nature of our perception and use of the category of time. If the human tendency is to concretize our rationality by exaggerating its spatiality, how ought theology conceive of its task of interpreting time? Certainly time has been a dominant feature of Western theology throughout the course of its history. The typological methodology utilized by the New Testament and early church theologians, for example, is grounded in a particular way of viewing time (the past foreshadows the present). Likewise, Christian apocalyptic speculation (the future foreshadowed in the present) moved from its infancy in the New Testament to the elaborate images of the early and later Middle Ages. Has not time, then, been integrated into the heart of the Christian tradition consistently throughout the history of theology? An affirmative answer, I believe, can only be substantiated in a very specific way. Time has indeed played a key role in traditional Christian thought, but only in a spatialized sense. Thus, it is important to understand Christian thought typically as either spatializing time or timing space. In either instance, time traditionally has been captured by Christian thinkers and utilized as a fundamental part of the landscape of Christian space, whether that be the landscape of this world or the one to come. The thrust here is to conceive of time in a very narrow way: it is to lock it in to established spatially conceived patterns and configurations. Calvinism, with its doctrine of predestination, itself a theological tradition of enormous implications for American thought, is only an extreme example of this general tendency of Western (European-based) theology.

The result of this constricted theology is that time has not been free to achieve its full theological significance in the Western cultural sphere. We must, it seems, liberate time from the boundaries of our space. America, as a product of Western thought, has been especially susceptible to this restricted utilization of the time concept. Because of the theological foundation of much of its culture, and the ongoing public function of religion, the truncated perception of time has had extreme consequences for American society as a whole. What has not been taken into account sufficiently is the artificial way we intellectually grasp time. Time, like space, is not simply *there*. Rather, like the whole of nature,[10] it is an idea that compels the subject to participate in the construction of its meaning. Time, in other words, is not a given; it is itself fundamentally hermeneutical in

---

[10]For a discussion of the idea that a society imprints upon nature those categories that are dominant in its social life, see Mary Douglas, *Implicit Meanings: Essays in Anthropology* (London: Routledge and Kegan Paul, 1975).

character. This fact has the highest significance and itself calls for further interpretation. The matter is summarized quite succinctly by the Belgian scientist Ilya Prigogine: "Today we know that time is a construction and therefore carries an ethical responsibility."[11] The way we perceive time, and, more to the point, the way we use time, carries the strongest moral implication. Certainly, we must make something out of the experience of life and death, summer and winter, and the like. But how we do this is a question of many dimensions. Similarly, how we relate time to space is also a problem of profound importance in the way we perceive all of life. And, it is precisely this "all of life" that makes the whole matter a religious concern, and of the highest significance for our well-being.

This particular study of American biblical hermeneutics has addressed the issue of the restructuring of our concepts of space and time. Because these concepts fundamentally underlie all other intellectual categories, I understand this whole approach as being one concerned with the grammar of all our intellectual constructions. Furthermore, I see this work as one that displaces because it finally leads to the complete rethinking of the Christian position (role/place) in the cosmos (society/ world). Through the analysis of how our culturally conditioned understanding of time and space influences our reading of biblical texts, we hope to have achieved some insight into its ability to function creatively in our theology. This whole discussion of American biblical hermeneutics points to the need to create a new hermeneutical questioning of the Bible that displaces our culturally spatial one with another one that reprioritizes the problem of time. Only in this way can we restore a Bible possessing a reinvigorated voice, adequate to the challenge of the complex issues of New World religion, and beyond. To that end, it is helpful to explicate more precisely how the failure of satisfactorily reading American space and time has blunted the force and effect of American theology, and how that failure opens the way to American biblical hermeneutics.

Those theologians who have creatively contributed to our understanding of American religion have refused the pervasive anti-intellectual, unthinkingly protechnological traditions of American life that maintain a false "thinking or doing" dichotomy. They recognize that religion fundamentally entails a distinctive way of thinking about the world and humankind. They do not understand thinking as a secondary reflection on activity, or a derivative of doing, but as an activity coequal with doing. Thus, while the priority of praxis is generally taken for granted in American thought, it is also acknowledged that praxis includes thinking. With this preliminary thought, let us turn to a brief consideration of the work of two formative figures in the quest for an American theology, H.

---

[11]Ilya Prigogine, *Order Out of Chaos: Man's New Dialogue with Nature* (Toronto, New York: Bantam Books, 1984) 312.

Richard Niebuhr and Herbert Richardson, with an eye to how the very limitations of their approaches are uncovered by American biblical hermeneutics.

Following his acclaimed *The Social Sources of Denominationalism*, in 1937 H. Richard Niebuhr published an alternative approach to the study of American religious thought entitled *The Kingdom of God in America*. Whereas the previous work was a sociological study of American religious institutions, the latter was intended as an interpretive statement of the meaning of the history of American religion from the vantage point within, rather than without, the Christian faith.[12] In *The Kingdom of God in America*, Niebuhr acknowledges the danger in sociology of bringing external patterns of interpretation to the interpretive task and observes that the first study "left me dissatisfied at a number of points." He continues,

> Though the sociological approach helped to explain why the religious stream flowed in these particular channels it did not account for the force of the stream itself; while it seemed relevant enough to the institutionalized churches it did not explain the Christian movement which produced these churches; while it accounted for the diversity in American religion it did not explain the unity which our faith possesses despite its variety; while it could deal with the religion which was dependent on culture it left unexplained the faith which is independent, which is aggressive rather than passive, and which molds culture instead of being molded by it.[13]

The Kingdom of God in America was intended to correct the flaws indicated in this passage.[14] It is a work intended to explicate the interior dynamic force of the Christian faith. This text is particularly important in that it sets the stage for a modern approach to American theology independent of both liberal and conservative approaches that too easily attempt to unite the American experience with a particular reading of the Bible. Important in Niebuhr's approach is the refusal to identify God's kingdom with any earthly manifestation of human rule, whether it be political, economic, or

---

[12]H. Richard Niebuhr, *The Kingdom of God in America* (New York: Harper & Row, 1937) 12.

[13]Ibid., ix–x.

[14]In this statement, Niebuhr drives home his argument with the sociological approach to American religion: "When we turn to the history of American Christianity in particular we are scarcely convinced by the arguments of social historians that a John Cotton, a Roger Williams, a Jonathan Edwards, a Channing and all the other reputed initiators of new movements were primarily representatives of social loyalties. For the kingdom of God to which these men and the movements they initiated were loyal was not simply American culture or political and economic interest exalted and idealized; it was rather a kingdom which was prior to America and to which this nation, in its politics and economics, was required to conform" (ibid., 10).

otherwise. In a very real sense, American theology begins with the rejection of the identity of American society with God's rule made by naive faith. This is the theological legacy upon which American biblical hermeneutics builds, and which permeates every aspect of its own development. American culture is not one and the same with God's rule; they may be dialectically related, but not identified. This crucial insight, already clearly present in Niebuhr's work, makes it an appropriate text in the development toward American biblical hermeneutics.

In his reading of the history of American religious thought, Niebuhr was deeply influenced by Continental neo-orthodoxy and its proposal of a dialectical theology.[15] This theological tradition itself was deeply grounded in biblical thought. He believed to have discovered the interpretive key to this history in the integrative Protestant concept of the Kingdom of God. The specific content of this idea varied throughout its development on American soil: "If the seventeenth was the century of the sovereignty [of God] and the eighteenth the time of the kingdom of Christ, the nineteenth may be called the period of the coming kingdom."[16] Nonetheless, the enveloping concept represented a coherent theological movement. At one point he describes its reverberations through American history in allegorical terms.

> The kingdom of God in America is neither an ideal nor an organization. It is a movement which, like the city of God described by Augustine in ancient time, appears in only partial and mixed manner in the ideas and institutions in which men seek to fix it. In that movement we vaguely discern a pattern—one which is not like the plan of a building or any static thing, but more like the pattern of a life, a poem or of other things dynamic. It is a New World symphony in which each movement has its own specific theme, yet builds on all that has gone before and combines with what follows so that the meaning of the whole can be apprehended only as the whole is heard.[17]

Since the Protestant movement had framed and animated the American experience, Niebuhr begins his interpretation with a brief analysis of it. Although Protestantism is European in origin, it is also "America's only national religion."[18] One crucial aspect of Protestantism, however, distinguishes the American version from the European movement. In America, Niebuhr believed that "Protestantism could turn from protest

---

[15]Ibid., xiv–xv.

[16]Ibid., 150.

[17]Ibid., 164.

[18]Quoted by Niebuhr, in André Siegfried, *America Comes of Age*, trans. H. H. Hemming and Doris Hemming (New York: Harcourt, Brace, and Co., 1927) 33.

and conflict to construction."[19] America, in other words, would be the place where Protestantism would unfold in accordance with its own intrinsic dynamism, developing out of the original, revitalizing movement in the Continental context of Catholicism and state church. In this sense, America had the destiny of becoming more Protestant than Protestantism itself.

The constant companion of American Protestantism was the danger that it would fall victim to its foes on the right and the left: the former falling victim to the identification of the Kingdom of God with absolute monarchical, capitalistic, democratic, or socialistic powers; the latter relinquishing their adherence to absolutes altogether. Niebuhr's text is intended to discredit both of these tendencies. But, because of his own past close associations with liberalism, and its popularity in his own day, it was this version of Christianity that receives his greatest criticism.

> The coming kingdom of late liberalism, like the heaven of senile orthodoxy, came to be a place not of liberty and glory but of material delights, the modern counterparts of those pleasures which it had laughed to scorn when it spoke of ancient superstitions. For the golden harps of the saints it substituted radios, for angelic wings concrete highways and high-powered cars, and heavenly rest was now called leisure. But it was all the same old pattern; only the symbols had changed.[20]

Within only a few years after the Great Depression, it is not surprising that this is one of the few passages in the book that explicitly addresses the relationship between religion and commercialized technology. Again, the central point was to distinguish Christianity from Americanism. Only from the Christian context could the judgment be proclaimed with its call for repentance. Only from a belief in God and his forgiveness could nationality itself, even Christianity particularized in a nation, be creative rather than destructive.[21] In order to safeguard this crucial distinction, Niebuhr maintained the importance of beginning the study of the history of American Christianity with the religion itself, rather than with American culture.[22] Only in this way could the inherent capacity of Christianity to shape culture, and not merely be shaped by it, be manifest.

Although Niebuhr fundamentally established the independence of American religious thought from that of the general culture, he failed to extricate it from a metaphysics established methodologically upon geographical space. Although a systematic theologian by training, and a self-

---

[19]Ibid., 43.

[20]Ibid., 196.

[21]Ibid., xvi.

[22]Ibid., 14.

proclaimed amateur in the history of American religion,[23] Niebuhr conceived of his subject as being defined by those religious figures and events occurring within the spatial boundaries of the United States. Time is methodologically important in the sense that Niebuhr is vitally interested in historical development. Time and space intersect only in the historical drama of religion played out in the American place: traditional categories of the academic study of American church history. In this regard, Niebuhr describes Christianity as a "movement or life directed toward the ever transcendent."[24] By definition, American religion becomes whatever *this* particular people make of it. The question is from this standpoint, what has American religion been, and where is it going? The question for American biblical hermeneutics is, what *ought* American religion be, and what is its potential? For the academic American church historian, time is a given factor of the unfolding of history. Time is viewed in spatial terms, in the sense of the place of the progression of the American religious experience. In this traditional sense, it is incumbent upon the historian to record how the space is taken up and upon the theologian to find some meaning in it all.

It is during his discussion of the nineteenth century and its aftermath, interpreted under the theme of "The Coming Kingdom," that Niebuhr specifically addresses a fundamental way of interpreting time within the American experience. In America, he notes, "the faith in its coming was transformed into a belief in progress."[25] Niebuhr correctly opposes this way of utilizing time from a Christian perspective. In reality, the idea of progress is often nothing more than an ideological defense used as a strategy of maintaining the status quo: "Don't look at the way things are, but by what they are becoming." But, the criticism remains: Is not his own concept of a "movement or life directed toward the ever transcendent" only a more sophisticated conception of time that is grounded on the same metaphysical properties as that of progress? He really imbues the course of American religious development with manifest theological significance: "This may seem to be an effort to present theology in the guise of history, yet the theology has grown out of the history as much as the history has grown out of the theology."[26] In this perspective, time is truncated into the rational construction of past, present, and future, so that it can be more easily managed in its application to the North American continent. But what of Jesus' statement, "Behold, the Kingdom of God is at hand?" How are we to relate this perspective on time to the American ex-

---

[23]Ibid., x.

[24]Ibid., xiv.

[25]Ibid., 183.

[26]Ibid., xiii.

perience? Only when we can satisfactorily accomplish this may an American theology be compelling and concrete.

In 1967, with the publication of *Toward an American Theology*, Herbert W. Richardson instigated the search for an "American theology" in what he termed the new "sociotechnic age."[27] Although the reviews were mixed with regard to Richardson's exploratory ideas (as he, himself, designated them[28]), I believe that this text remains the formative one in the effort self-consciously to take the American experience as a theological category. As such, it stands programmatically in the immediate background of American biblical hermeneutics and establishes fundamental categories of American theological discourse. However, as helpful and penetrating as Richardson's approach is for this material, it is flawed in certain ways that American biblical hermeneutics can correct. Therefore, it is beneficial to examine briefly both the strengths and weaknesses of this text from the standpoint of what might be accomplished by the new way of reading the Bible that is promised by American biblical hermeneutics.

Writing in the 1960s, during the height of the so-called radical theology period, Richardson maintained that American atheism was a product of the inability of the dominant form of American Christianity—imported European Protestantism—to cope with the new realities of American culture. He saw his time as one of transition to a fundamentally new cultural epoch, with atheism serving in the prophetic category of calling attention to the inadequacies of the tradition. He programmatically set forth his task in these terms:

> The task of theology is not only to affirm the new concerns implied by the prophetic atheism of a transitional moment in history, but also to resist their secularization. In providing a religious integration for a new intellectus, theology also works to redeem that intellectus from the destructive power of secularism. In the following essay I shall take up this problem, giving special attention to the peculiar form of secular idolatry that threatens to distort or destroy the sociotechnical intellectus of the coming age.[29]

This text makes the crucial point in Richardson's approach that the "sociotechnical intellectus"[30] is not to be identified with "secular idolatry."

---

[27]Richardson, *Toward an American Theology* (New York: Harper & Row, 1967).

[28]Ibid., 161.

[29]Ibid., 29.

[30]Richardson discusses the term *sociotechnics* in this way: "The reason for calling this new movement sociotechnics rather than technology is to oppose the popular theory that technology is intrinsically related to natural science. We so frequently encounter the phrase 'science and technology' that we have come to think of technology as the fruit of scientific endeavor. But this is not the case. Technology uses science in the same way Newton used Arabic numerals and

Before the dawning period, such secular idolatries as "economic man," "scientific man," and "political man" had attempted whole interpretations of human experience without God. The new sociotechnical age was as much a threat to these secular interpretations as it was to traditional Christian thought. If Christian theology could meet the inevitable challenge of this new intellectual movement, then, perhaps, the latter might be spared a new process of secularization. In summary, Richardson's purpose was to show precisely how American culture had exceeded the intellectual boundaries of Protestantism and to suggest ways in which an adequate understanding of the faith might be both retrieved from the ecumenical Christian tradition and enlarged and reshaped to address the new challenge of the age. The purpose of this approach was to protect both the Christian faith and technology from the dangers of the radical secularization of the times.

The key to Richardson's American theology lies in his acceptance of the inevitability of the dominance of technology in our time throughout the world. This position is set against the background that technology itself is universal and crosses all cultural boundaries; therefore, nothing specifically American about it exists per se. What brings the American question to the fore is the long-term symbiosis of Americans with technology. Richardson quotes from Max Lerner:

> The Big Technology has been for Americans what the Cross was for the Emperor Constantine: *in hoc signo vincas* [*sic*]. It set the pace for an impressively swift and thorough conquest of a new environment and of world leadership. The American has been a machine-intoxicated man. The love affair (it has been nothing less) between the Americans and their Big Technology has been fateful, for it has joined the impersonal power of the machine to the dynamism of the American character. As by some tropism of the spirit, the Americans have followed out the logic of technology all the way.[31]

America is characterized among world civilizations by an unabashed faith in technology. In developing this point, Richardson maintains that since no society has such a close relationship with the spirit of the coming age as America, then it follows that, of all societies, America can offer the greatest resources in helping formulate an adequate Christian response

---

computation procedures. Technology is not created by science; it is the invention, rather, of those social thinkers who sought not to advance science but to create a new form of social organization. This desire to create a new social organization is what differentiates contemporary sociotechnology from the *techne* of the ancient Greeks" (ibid., 17).

[31]Ibid., 27–28. See Max Lerner, "Big Technology and Neutral Technicians," in Hendrik M. Ruitenbeck, *The Dilemma of Organizational Society*, (New York: Dutton, 1963) 77–78.

to it.

Richardson makes his case for an American theology, therefore, on the fundamental basis that if Americans are "machine-intoxicated," then theologians should study this society for basic insights into the human interaction with the machine.

> My proposal that Christianity affirm and shape a sociotechnical intellectus is not based on any preference for this intellectus, but on a recognition of its inevitability. Theology need not fear to move in this direction, for it is not confined to any particular cultural expression, *but is rooted in a divine revelation.* Just as, from the perspective of this revelation, theology has previously shaped a Christian Platonism, a Christian Aristotelianism, and a Christian individualism, so it can and will shape a Christian sociotechnicism. Theology can do this because it is rooted in a revelation which contains the fullness of truth and because it knows that every created intellectus is a partial expression of that fullness [my emphasis].[32]

The crucial point here is that technology is accepted as a given in the emerging world, not because of its inherent intellectual superiority, but because of its inevitability.[33] This is a time-oriented word, one that gives a dominant role to the future. Since the future determines what will be, it is useless to fight against what it mandates. The task for the theologian, therefore, is to take the given materials of "revealed truth" (which, presumably, stand outside time) and reshape them for each newly appearing cultural setting and epoch in which they are found. This is to be done, not because the setting and epoch are bad in and of themselves, but so that they might be saved from the forces of secularization. America is selected for a special role in theology because it is more in tune with the (inevitable) future than any other world civilization.[34] Therefore, Richardson

---

[32]Richardson, *Toward an American Theology*, 29.

[33]On the question of inevitability, Richardson writes, "In their sustained opposition to the cybernetic revolution of our time, many liberal critics reveal a surprisingly unhistorical attitude. They do not even acknowledge the inevitability of the transformation that is taking place. This transformation is inevitable because the knowledge of the sociotechnics is more powerful than the old arts and sciences of the modern world, and is capable of helping us to deal with critical problems of our age—problems the modern world has generated but has not been able to solve. The cultural transformation that is taking place is therefore as inevitable as the transformation of Augustinian culture under the impact of Islamic science or the transformation of late medieval culture under the impact of individualism and the empirical sciences. A more profound and penetrating rationality has been discovered, and the 'modern intellectus' is being overthrown by it" (ibid., 20).

[34]Concerning the dominant place of the future in American thought, Richardson correctly notes, "It is still true that what is uniquely characteristic of America is not what she shares with modern Europe, but her faith in social technology.

conceives of Christian thought as an arm of the general Christian redemptive movement, with the American cultural experience providing a major resource in this movement.

The focus on chronological inevitability in Richardson's work means that he recognizes the central place of an interpretation of time on a surface level. But, like Niebuhr, he fails to penetrate to the needed hermeneutics of time for which the Christian faith calls. Does not the very conceptual framework of chronological inevitability itself call for investigation in terms of further development of the theology of history implied within it? As a result, although many of the individual points he makes are valid and ground breaking, especially his interest in addressing theologically the question of technology, the metaphysical framework evident in his interpretation results in a truncated view of time. In fact, in this book Richardson finds no way of escaping the common practice of utilizing time on behalf of a certain view of (American) space. As such, chronological inevitability becomes little more than a synonym for "the American way." America is the place where the future is most clearly visible in the present; therefore, by definition, America assumes a preferable position vis-à-vis other cultures. In Richardson's approach, this is the reason the inevitability factor is so crucial. In short, chronological inevitability establishes cultural hegemony—time serving space by means of a deterministic preunderstanding ("the future must be. . . ."). Richardson's underlying metaphysics of (geographical) space becomes evident in the course of the book. For example, he writes,

> *Western* European Christianity places a disproportionate emphasis on the New Testament, especially the Pauline writings, and therefore fails to give an adequate place to Old Testament teaching. It ascribes to the doctrine of sin a centrality that leads to a distorted understanding of the person and work of Jesus Christ. Its norms for understanding human life are drawn primarily from a theory of nature rather than from an understanding of the world as God's creation. It has displaced the Trinity from its proper place in the life of faith. It has neglected the work of the Holy Spirit and the communal life of the Church as God's present kingdom. . . . I acknowledge from the outset a resemblance which many European commentators have also mentioned: that American Christianity shares with Judaism its theocratic emphasis and that, in the last analysis, its spiritualistic interpretation of the Christian faith in terms of worship and incarnation (rather than sin and crucifixion) binds American religion more closely to Orthodoxy than to the *western* Church [my emphasis].[35]

The vision of a wholly artificial environment, man and society together restructured by the power of the machine, is the American dream. And Christian eschatology has undergirded and sustained this dream from the earliest beginnings of our life as a nation" (ibid., 28).

[35]Ibid., 111–12.

This description of American Christian thought is framed in the spatial image of *Western* European Christianity, a form of the faith held in distinction to Judaism and Orthodoxy. The accuracy or inaccuracy of this descriptive statement of what has historically characterized American religion does not concern us here. What is important is the way of thinking that this text indicates and the implications of this thinking for the fuller scope of theology.

What is lacking in Richardson's American theology is the critical perspective that a hermeneutical perspective of time provides. America is not merely a place that is subject to historical movement and development: time is an essential part of the fabric of the American experience from its inception. America is just as much an experiment in time, an interpretation of time, as it is of geographical space. A certain way of understanding time is integral to the invention of America from its inception. This is the deeper level of interpretation that the Bible calls upon us to penetrate. Because America chooses a love affair with "Big Technology," this choice is not given validity by reference to historical necessity. Perhaps this is a false choice, a mistake that needs to be corrected. It is incumbent upon American biblical hermeneutics to evaluate this choice because the writers of the Bible (especially evident in the Old Testament) evaluated similar decisions within their cultural contexts.

To develop a theory of cultural superiority on the basis of futurity is to ignore that the very concept of futurity itself is already an interpretation of time, replete with underlying presuppositions, that is framed within a particular cultural setting. While it is possible to predict the future, nothing is absolutely inevitable. Furthermore, the concept of chronological inevitability carries the implication of a future that is more real than the past or present. In reality, all three—past, present, and future—are rational constructions of the phenomenon of time. Only by recognizing this can a genuinely critical theology be developed—a theology that is equally critical of human perceptions of past, present, and future. Even if the argument of chronological inevitability is overpowering within a particular historical context, such an argument is no guarantor of truth. Because something will surely be does not mean that it ought to be. To fail to make this fundamental distinction is to rid time of its ethical dimension and the recognition of our own participation in the construction of its meaning. The resultant narrow view of time has the effect of the loss of critical perspective: how, precisely, is the culture to become aware of the otherness of the biblical heritage, and at what point is the biblical heritage to stand opposed to the culture? The liberation of time from its utilization in the support of space ("this is so because it has always been so," "this is ours because it was meant to be ours," and the like) is the first step in the appropriation of the American experience as a theological category. Only in this way, by recognizing that the biblical view of time may be quite different than a particular cultural perspective, may we genuinely speak of a dialogue between culture and religion and not the dictation of one to the other.

Richardson's assumptions may be summarized as follows:

1) The revelation of Christian truth and fundamental theological categories.

2) The recognition of the determinative "intellectus" of a particular culture in a particular time.

3) The integration of the fundamental theological categories the particular determinative "intellectus."

The end result of this scheme is the redemption of the culture through the shaping and forming power of Christian thought. As an unfolding of this activity, one would expect that theology itself also becomes enriched. In distinction to Richardson's approach, American biblical hermeneutics makes three assumptions:

1) The apprehension of penetrating cultural critiques of the "American mind" in the context of the recognition that all cultural forms are the product of a series of ethical choices rooted in space and time.

2) The utilization of that critical vision as an interpretive tool in re-reading the source document of Christian thought (the Bible) as a means of manifesting new meaning.

3) The unfolding of this movement in the broader theological context. The primary purpose of this model is the manifestation of a more meaningful theology that addresses the realities and potentialities of the American setting. In addition, because a public hermeneutics already transcends sacred/secular barriers by incorporating both realms, the dominant intellectual currents peculiar to the culture become significantly enriched through the critical process. Richardson ultimately falls victim to reducing Christian theology to a position of secondary importance within the prevailing American cultural ethos. He presupposes that the culture is inevitably headed in a certain direction and that Christian thought must conform and adapt in order to make a meaningful response. American biblical hermeneutics is more critical of the direction of the society because the Bible forces it to be so.

In summary, the problem visible throughout these and other approaches to American theology has been the failure to recognize the revolutionary shift in theology called for by the American technological experience delineated by Mumford, Orwell, Ellul, and many others. In particular, influenced by their own training and their colleagues in the academic setting, American theologians typically remain bound to American space. What remains is an uncovering of an American theology rooted in the depth dimensions of the dialectic of place and time: that time has been just as much a product of the American imagination as has its space. The spatialization of American thought tends toward a reactionary intellectual environment that holds our religious traditions in an exterior and objective mode of existence. Here, theology is set primarily in reaction to

European Christianity. The recasting of theology in temporal categories brings the promise of an interior reading of these traditions that is praxical and subjective in a particularistic way. In this mode, theology is liberated from its own pastness and open to the impulses of its own setting in life. It is not to be expected that the plumbing of the interior features of one's own ethnic psyche is painless. Like a surgical procedure, the right intellectual tools are needed, tools that are promised by the dialectics of American biblical hermeneutics.

• Delocalizing American Theology •

American biblical hermeneutics is the redefinition of the quest for theology in America by making explicit the hermeneutical features already present within it. Unlike apodictic theological approaches, this one maintains an open dialectical aspect that invites newness and creativity. In discussing what he terms "deep reading," Richard R. Niebuhr writes,

> The art of reading deeply is also an unending conflict between convention and innovation. It is the interpolation of the text or passage into the reader's experience and the reader's experience into the passage, not, to be sure, either haphazardly or according to rigid rules but tactfully and experimentally.
>
> In such reading we no longer *encounter* the text. We *dwell* in it, and the text *dwells* in us. But deep reading is still more lively and complex: for we are continuously stepping in and out of this voluminous space, now regarding its written symbols from the "outside" as though inscribed on a facade and now living and exploring in their midst [author's emphasis].[36]

To dwell in the biblical text, and have it dwell in us, is the goal of our study. When this relationship between reader and text is an indwelling, the more profound the relatedness and its results. It is this dwelling in the text that American biblical hermeneutics wishes to achieve, rather than merely reading it objectively. This can only be achieved by bringing the subjective aspect of reading into full self-consciousness. In this process the reader does not lose him/herself completely. The text always remains text, and the reader always remains reader. A critical distance between the two is necessarily there and should be self-consciously recognized. But the self-conscious encounter between them, if the text is a classic one, carries the reader to a new place. This is not exactly the place where the text is, but it is a place different from the one where the reader began.

I have argued that the urgent task of theology in this culture is to push critically beyond the contours of *placeness* to one that addresses directly the prior problem of *time*. It is its involvement with time that helps make "America" a theological category of universal dimensions, pushing the

---

[36]Richard R. Niebuhr, "The Strife of Interpreting: The Moral Burden of Imagination," *Parabola* 10:2 (May 1985): 39–40.

meaning of the concept beyond the political boundaries of its space in the world.[37] The traditional tie to the primacy of space/place in the attempts to understand America has its roots in a false metaphysics that continues to undergird most of our thinking. We need to think beyond it to the chronological implications implicit in the phraseology "*New World.*" The way this term is embedded in American consciousness is itself informed by the Bible (*Old* Testament/*New* Testament). Is not America the "New Testament," and Europe the "Old"? The early experience of America for its formative thinkers was a spiritual one that carried along with it a new way of thinking as well. The watery chaos of the Atlantic Ocean presented a new type of exodus and Red Sea experience for colonial Americans, which led to innovative thinking that extended into more universal forms of thought. So too is the power of the American experience.

American theology restricted to a spatial America inadequately meets the critical challenge of the technological society. The failure to perceive this has stunted the organic development of American theology beyond its inception in American sociohistorical realities. As a result, it is necessary to reconceive our theology and give it new moorings. Initially, this involves the experience of *dis*placement of much that is familiar to us. When time is allowed its full intellectual force, it is itself a *displacing* reality. In the language of modern physics, we must strive for an authentic theology that is spacetime oriented. Spacetime is the removal of the absoluteness of space by the introduction of time into its inner fabric. No space is final and absolute. Space has the tendency of framing or capturing time, whereas time is the fluidity of space. The two concepts working together in dialectical relationship define the structure of human meaning. *How* we understand these categories establishes the content of human understanding. Theology, then, differs from more scientific pursuits in the sense that it attempts a rational explanation of that which cannot be verified through rational experience alone: the experience of displacement. While this experience of displacement is present in these primal activities of modern life, it is present in a much less direct and hidden way. Theology itself, however, attempts to provide a place for that which has been displaced. In this sense, theology is artificial, we may even say tech-

---

[37]Perhaps the definitive text here is the one from Crèvecoeur: "What then is the American, this man? He is either an European, or the descendant of an European, hence that strange mixture of blood, which you will find in no other country. . . . *He* is an American, who, leaving behind him all his ancient prejudices and manners, receives new ones from the new mode of life he has embraced, the new government he obeys, and the new rank he holds. . . . Americans are the western pilgrims, who are carrying along with them that great mass of arts, sciences, vigour, and industry which began long since in the east; they will finish the great circle" [author's emphasis]. J. Hector St. John de Crèvecoeur, *Letters from an American Farmer* (New York: E. P. Dutton, 1957) 39.

nological. The foundational role of American biblical hermeneutics is to give guidance to this task of redefining American theology initially, but contributing finally to the redefinition of theology as such.

In the categories of which I am speaking, culture is the establishment of place. It provides a locus of meaning within which the chaotic nature of raw experience can be set and interpreted by a definable group. Christian experience, however, refuses the imposed limitations peculiar to the place that culture provides. That is why Christianity is not to be identified with any particular culture and must struggle to transcend it even as it is grounded in it. Instead of existing within culture, or alongside culture, critical theology strives to engage culture from a critical distance. This means that it affirms it even as it sets it in a wholly new context. In this way, it is appropriate to think of Christianity as lifting up any particular culture and placing it in a different environment, an environment that *de*-absolutizes it. Once the experience of displacement has occurred, the dimension of time arises to fill or *re*place what was lost. Fundamentally, time is a mental construct generated by this activity of *re*placement. This is exhibited as forthrightly as possible in Jesus' prime, irreducible statement: "Behold, the Kingdom of God is at hand." Jesus speaks of a replacement of the Kingdom of God in this way: a statement that redefines God's activity from that of place (earthly kingdom) to that of time (at hand). This replacement of the conception of absolute space with that of space in relationship to time stands as the fundamental paradigm of Christian theology. It is here that American theology should begin, as indeed should theology in general. Clearly, American theology has ultimate significance only insofar as it participates fully in the overall task of theology.

The error of traditional American theology lies in its inability to deal adequately with this problem of the space and time of American culture; therefore, it has not shown an ability to express itself in terms that transcend its own particularity while remaining true to its inner meaning. Spatial theology is victimized by a provincial orientation that tethers it to a particular culture; a chronological theology easily moves to the universal questions of all cultures. The former remains, in short, a victim of the secular/sacred dichotomy present in Cartesian objectifying metaphysics that continues to burden Western thought in our day. It is still bound to the "historical sciences" that treat it as a thing, rather than an opportunity. American biblical hermeneutics is a direct attack upon this mentality in that it is a relational activity (American culture/biblical culture) rather than an objective one. It makes no pretensions of being absolutely comprehensive. As a result, American biblical hermeneutics is intended to be paradigmatic in terms of its relationship to other theological and philosophical activities. It strives for this paradigmatic status in the only authentic way possible in a truly pluralistic environment: by being relational within itself. This carries the implication that no one particular approach to American biblical hermeneutics is authoritative and determinative for the rest. The goal of this approach to theology is not to find the one, right interpretation of the Bible (an American approach, or the like). No such approach exists "out there" to be discovered by some insightful interpreter. Neither is there a method to be discovered. The particular shape and form of the relationship between text and reader, or culture and culture, depends on the particularities of the reader and his/her culture. Rather than striving for one approach to the Bible that will dominate and supersede all the rest, the intention here is to take the phenomenon of plurality of readings itself as a theological category. The worth of this or that particular method that is employed is judged fundamentally on the basis of the fruits of the method, that is to say, the quality of the theological reflection that it engenders. In this sense, the end does justify the means.

The combination of the terms *American/biblical/hermeneutics* points to a dynamic intellectual activity. One category is secular with sacred overtones (America), another is sacred with secular overtones (biblical text), and the third points to the relational character that exists between them and points to the activity of understanding that this relationship provokes (hermeneutics). No matter what particular shape and form hermeneutics takes, it signifies the relation between text and reader. Furthermore, it points to difficulties in that relationship even as it is engaged. As a result, problems associated with the Cartesian worldview that shaped the formation of American culture are of particular relevance to this activity. American biblical hermeneutics works against the Cartesian dichotomy, especially the tendency to understand it as absolute. Like philosophy, it encourages the theoretical implications to be drawn out of secularity and not remain hidden in the self-imposed ignorance of mindless activity. This is done so that those activities may be subjected to critical analysis and corrected in larger horizons of thought. In addition, while secular categories are rightly autonomous when they deal specifically with their own subject matter, they are not so when the implications of that subject matter begin to spill over into the general areas of human existence. At that precise moment when any specific secular discipline alters the fundamental way we understand ourselves and the world in which we live, then that discipline becomes a matter of theological signification. The burden of creative theology is the necessarily continual engagement of the secular, as well as the sacred. This conscious activity means that the pleasures of reflecting on the sacred alone are given up for the sake of the world, which we find ultimately is only another version of the sacred itself.

• NAME INDEX •

• SUBJECT INDEX •